O9-BUD-084

33

Social History of Canada

H.V. Nelles, general editor

雨情

TAKEO UJO NAKANO
WITH LEATRICE NAKANO

Within the barbed wire fence

A JAPANESE MAN'S

ACCOUNT OF HIS INTERNMENT

IN CANADA

With an Afterword by W. Peter Ward

University of Toronto Press
Toronto Buffalo London

© University of Toronto Press 1980
Toronto Buffalo London
Printed in Canada

Canadian Cataloguing in Publication Data

Nakano, Takeo, 1903-
Within the barbed wire fence

ISBN 0-8020-2382-7

1. Nakano, Takeo, 1903- 2. Japanese Canadians –
Evacuation and relocation, 1942-1945.* 3. Japanese
in Canada – Biography. I. Nakano, Leatrice, 1949-
II. Title.

FC106.J3N34   971'.004956   C80-094491-7
F1035.J3N34

FRONTISPIECE: The prize-winning tanka from the Imperial Poetry
Contest of 1964, in Takeo Nakano's calligraphy

Two of the photographs on page 27 (unloading coal, and visiting bear
cubs) are reproduced courtesy of C. Wakabayashi. The photographs
of the camp at Angler on pages 58, 60, and 79 are courtesy of Y.
Uyeda.

Contents

PREFACE vii
Prologue: Woodfibre days 3
Evacuation from Woodfibre 8
To Vancouver and on to Yellowhead road camp 12
Life at Yellowhead 19
To Descoigne road camp 25
Life at Descoigne 31
To Slocan instead of Greenwood 37
To jail in Vancouver 43
Transcontinental removal 50
First weeks at Angler 55
Adaptation difficulties 63
The haiku club 69
Winter shut-ins 76
A civilian casualty 82
Adaptation accomplished? 86
Decision to leave 91
Secret arrangements for departure 97
Epilogue: Toronto and a fresh start 101
AFTERWORD W. Peter Ward 109

Preface

THIS WORK has a long and varied history. It existed in embryo in Takeo Nakano's diary, interspersed with tanka verse, for the years 1942 and 1943, the time of the events he narrates. In the 1960s, Takeo worked on a prose account based upon the diary. In 1969 his *Sensei* (roughly 'oath of citizenship') was published in Japanese and in Japan, but intended for distribution mainly to Japanese Canadians. *Sensei* consists of nearly six hundred tanka, composed during the period from 1942 to the time of publication, and some seventy pages of prose. Since the decision at that time was to make the work essentially a book of tanka, only a fraction of the prose he had prepared was included.

By the mid-1970s Takeo had come to think that some of the content of *Sensei* might interest a non-Japanese Canadian audience. In 1975-6, with the aid of the Toronto Japanese Canadian Citizens Association, he applied for and received a translation grant from the Multiculturalism Directorate of the Secretary of State.

Kasey Oyama, of Montreal, was engaged to do the translation. He began work on *Sensei* and the prose text that had not been included in that work, and in time envisioned a potential new work which would amplify Takeo's somewhat sketchy account – sketchy because it had originally been aimed at an audience who had themselves experienced the evacuation or were otherwise familiar with it. He planned to draw from Takeo's memory more details with which to supplement the original. But it proved impracticable for him to work this closely with Takeo, because of problems of time and distance. He had, therefore, to content himself with rendering a direct translation of that original account, and I was invited to realize the book he had envisioned. I am the second of Takeo's two daughters. My sister Toshimi appears in the account, but I was not born until after the war.

With my father and mother I first made a translation orally, using as its basis the original translation by Kasey. As we worked along, we supplemented the account with details from my father's memory. I then confirmed through research the accuracy of the factual details underlying the account. Finally, I wrote linking material so as to produce a coherent narrative. At some point, my father and I decided that, since the focus of the work had changed, and since tanka suffers by translation, we would reduce the number of tanka substantially.

Such were the stages in bringing the work to its present form.

A few words must be said about the account itself. It bears repeating that it is the account of one man. And that man is an Issei or first-generation Japanese in Canada. (This is as opposed to his being a Nisei or second-generation Japanese in Canada, i.e., a Canadian by birth, of Japanese descent.) Further, it must be said that the account is not that of one of the more typical internees at Angler internment camp, where most of the account is set. In my father's opinion the prevailing sentiment of the internees there was that of the *gambariya* (a term explained in the text), a sentiment to which he did not subscribe. The representation of the *gambariya* is thus clearly from an external point of view, and we alone take responsibility for that representation.

This account, whose embryo was the diary my father kept at the time of the events, is a true account in essence. Some omissions and alterations have been effected, however, in some cases in the interests of anonymity, in other cases to sharpen the focus on the protagonist and his experiences.

A final word about the forms of poetry that my father wrote. The tanka has a long tradition, as described in Professor Ward's Afterword. Its composition hinges on the poet's skill in expressing his thoughts in the established format: thirty-one syllables arranged in five lines of five, seven, five, seven, and seven respectively. It is not as well known in the West as the haiku, which has a simpler structure: seventeen syllables arranged in three lines of five, seven, and five. Yet the haiku is derived from the tanka, and emerged as an independent form only after the Meiji Restoration of 1868.

There are many acknowledgments, some for efforts dating back a number of years, and I shall make them in chronological order. Acknowledgments for administering the grant are due to these members of the Toronto Japanese Canadian Citizens Association: George Imai, Rits Inouye, Mits Sumiya, George Takahashi. Acknowledgments are also due to Joy Kogawa and to Dr Toyomasa Fuse, who helped initiate the project by finding Kasey Oyama. Robert Peter Willson, of Toronto, gave invaluable help in the research and in the later revisions. Many others, private individuals and staff members of various government departments, institutions, and libraries, kindly gave assistance in research. I thank Gerald Hallowell, H. Vivian Nelles, and W. Peter Ward for their efforts and encouragement, and Ian Montagnes for his sensitive and skilful editing. Finally, special thanks are given to Yukie Nakano and Robert Peter Willson without whose moral support this work would not have been possible.

This book has been published with the assistance of the Canada Council and the Ontario Arts Council under their programs of block grants to publishers.

LEATRICE NAKANO
Toronto
March 1980

Within the barbed wire fence

Prologue: Woodfibre days

WHEN THE WORLD is at war, it seems to me, blind forces are at work behind the scenes. All other considerations become secondary to the will to win, and armies of people do their utmost to hurt, if not to destroy, each other.

The second world war led the people of Japanese ancestry in Canada along a strange and difficult course, quite apart from the mainstream of the Canadian experience; but having struggled along it we find ourselves perhaps better for the experience. Yet I should not speak for others as I cannot say that my experience was typical of Japanese Canadians. Even those who travelled the same route as I did not always react in the same way. Often when I despaired, others were lighthearted. Each of us has his individual threshold of feeling. I think it not amiss, however, to present an account based upon my diary of the time.

I will never forget the date – March 16, 1942. It was almost one hundred days after Japanese bombs had fallen on Pearl Harbor. On that day all Japanese nationals (and therefore 'enemy aliens') in Woodfibre, BC, male and aged eighteen to forty-five inclusive, had been ordered to proceed to Vancouver, thence to road camps somewhere in the interior of British Columbia. Being a Japanese national and just under forty, I was one of the first group of evacuees. It was thus my fate to be parted from my wife and our eight-year-old girl and to face an uncertain future.

In retrospect, my life had been quite uneventful up to that point. After boyhood in a small farming town in Japan, in 1920, in my mid-teens, I had come to Canada with the dream of some day owning a big farm. I had gone to work on my uncle's berry farm near Hammond, BC. But the postwar economic decline had cut short my employment after just over two years. I had then gone to work at the Woodfibre Mill of the British Columbia Pulp and Paper Company.

Woodfibre, looking out over the quiet waters of Howe Sound, was an isolated company town some thirty miles up the coast from Vancouver and accessible only by water. Japanese, the majority of them single men, comprised roughly half the population of one thousand.

Woodfibre remains in my memory as an idyllic town where the Japanese lived in their tight little community in one section, the whites doing likewise in a better section. There were amicable if not close relations between the Japanese community and the white. They met regularly for the baseball game that took place each Sunday afternoon from spring into summer. Each community cheered enthusiastically for its team.

I accepted the fact that the whites were the elite. Their men were paid more than we were when they did the same jobs. Mainly they held the better jobs involving more specialized work. The majority of Japanese immigrant workers, myself included, spoke no English. The Japanese labour contractor, who did speak English, decided who would be hired and did all the negotiating with the company for us.

The high point of the year for the Japanese community was its annual Christmas variety show. On these occasions the drama group presented traditional theatre, such as parts of *The Forty-seven Ronin*. The honoured guest at this event was the plant manager. E.P. Brennan was to the Japanese more than a good employer. His warm speech initiated a very enjoyable evening. And he shook hands with many of us as he left the hall.

The monotony of our work was broken once a month when a Japanese freighter docked at Woodfibre to take on a load of wood pulp. The sawmill section was shut down, and all the Japanese workers were assigned to pulp-loading duties. White workers were not involved in this operation. It usually took about forty-eight hours to complete the job: two alternating shifts worked round the clock. The work was dangerous. Once when a load of pulp bales came crashing down from the ship's crane, sending workers scattering, one did not get out of the way in time. The mill whistle blew frantically. But the man was beyond help.

Fortunately, the loading was generally without mishap. And although the work was strenuous, my heart got a lift whenever I looked up and saw the blazing red sun of the Japanese flag waving reassuringly in the breeze. On the evening of the first day of each loading, the community would gather to hear the ship's officers speak. They had the latest news from Japan. Our Japanese consciousness, in constant danger of becoming sluggish from lack of stimulation, received a new transfusion from each prized contact with the fatherland.

In 1930 I made a short trip to Japan and returned married. Then I resumed working at the mill, and my wife taught at the Japanese language school. Gradually the onetime dream of the big farm was relinquished as the unrealistic ambition it had always been. But a new dream came to replace the old. We began sending our savings to be banked in Japan. Accordingly, well into the second decade of my employment as a mill hand, I felt ready for the next phase of my life. In a few years our

Yukie, Toshimi, and Takeo Nakano, in Woodfibre before evacuation

savings would be enough for us to return to Japan and establish ourselves there.

Meanwhile life in Woodfibre was good. One event, which stands out in my mind, was the Japanese community's celebration of the coronation of King George VI. An elaborate costume parade in the afternoon. A gala variety show in the evening. Men, women, children, all participated with fanatic fervour; our outpouring of loyalty to the new sovereign was surely not surpassed elsewhere in Canada.

But I think that the quieter environs of Woodfibre were nearest my heart; it seemed that nature had picked them to be her hiding place, which I was privileged to share.

Throughout the spring and into the summer, the peace that reigned in the wooded heights behind our town tempted me to solitary walks. How brilliant was the fresh light green of spring foliage, splashed against the sombre green of the conifers! I knew the spots where the trees thinned out and retreated, re-

vealing secluded glades strewn with dandelions, violets, colum-
bines, jack-in-the-pulpits, wood lilies, phlox, yellowbells,
blooming in careless profusion. And I quickly learned just
where to find the hidden patches of juicy wild strawberries.

With autumn came the suppressed excitement of the
mushroom hunt, deep in the woods. The pine mushrooms, as
difficult to find and as precious as buried treasure, had an
unmistakable piquant smell. Out in the sun, scarlet leaves
flickered fiery patterns against the mountainside. Autumn was
also the time when the waters before us summoned the men to
salmon fishing. Salmon that delighted us at the supper table!
We would see a hundred lights from the fishing vessels, undu-
lating in a sea of mysterious darkness. The beauty of this night
scene defied capture in words.

With the coming of winter, the mountains behind our town
were transformed into silent sentinels who would guard nature's domain until the stirring of a new spring.

I was not unmoved by all this beauty. I struggled with
words and phrases to find expression for the emotions that
stirred within me. I took up with renewed vigour the composition of tanka and haiku, whose rudiments I had learned in my
early teens; my life was infused with a new joy.

But one Sunday morning the peace of my existence was
shattered. Bombs fell on Pearl Harbor.

Evacuation from Woodfibre

PEARL HARBOR, the opening strike of the Japan-U.S. conflict, shocked Woodfibre's inhabitants. The quiet town was completely transformed as rumours propagated rumours, fed by often conflicting reports. The Japanese community especially was in an uproar.

We Japanese, largely working-class immigrants, were, generally speaking, not given to sophisticated political thinking. Rather we had in common a blind faith in Japan's eventual victory. The extent of our reasoning, decidedly specious in retrospect, was something like this: The burst of energy at Pearl Harbor was exemplary. If the war were short, say of less than two years' duration, Japan stood to win. If it were prolonged, Japan, weakened by over a decade of aggression in Manchuria and China, admittedly might lose. Meanwhile, we kept receiving reports of Japanese victories in the Far East. We therefore resolved to bear the present uneasiness patiently.

In the weeks that followed, life in Woodfibre was indeed changed. I remember especially the compulsory nightly blackout, meant to thwart the activity of Japanese bombers that might fly over British Columbia. With Canadians thus anx-

ious, some drastic move was inevitable. By mid-January of
1942, some of us faced the prospect of evacuation. At that
time it was said that if the Issei (Japanese-born) men aged
eighteen to forty-five went to the road camps, then the Issei
men over forty-five, the Issei women and children, and all
Nisei (Canadian-born of Japanese descent) would be allowed to
remain where they were. We Issei men accordingly received
an order to depart on March 16.

As the day of departure drew nearer, tension mounted in the
Japanese community. The lot of us Issei men was held to be a
sorry one indeed. The Rockies were terribly cold in March;
some of us would likely freeze to death in the twenty-below
temperature. Again, the steep mountains were subject to ava-
lanches; road work in them would be very dangerous. And
again, deep in the mountains, men could easily become isolated
by the snow and starve when provisions failed to get through
to them. With such conjectures, the families of Issei men
spent anxious days and sleepless nights. But the order to depart
was a government order. To accept it as fate was our sorry
resolve.

For now, the Canadian government seemed to regard as
'dangerous' only those who were Japanese nationals and men
of military age. It was thought that the removal of these men,
to beyond a hundred miles inland from the coast, would quiet
the anti-Japanese British Columbians, provincial government
officials prominent among them. (British Columbia had had a
history of anti-Japanese incidents since early in the century.
Mass immigration to one area by any ethnic group commonly
results in its unpopularity with the indigenous group. And
Japanese immigration to Canada had centred from the start in
British Columbia.) At any rate, at first only partial evacuation
was ordered. But the anti-Japanese element in the province
seized the opportunity to agitate. And concurrently the federal
government seemed to decide that this chance to solve the

long-standing 'Japanese problem' could not be passed up. Thus six weeks later complete evacuation was ordered. Eventually every person of Japanese descent, whether Japanese national or naturalized Canadian or Canadian-born citizen, whether male or female, whether adult or child, was to be evacuated.

Meanwhile March 16 arrived. In the late afternoon the Woodfibre dockside was crowded with our wives and our children, seeing us off. It was one great confusion. Concern about the uncertain future compounded the anxiety of parting. Both those who were seeing loved ones off and those who were being seen off had cheeks wet with involuntary tears.

The ferry awaited us. It was the one that made the daily run from Vancouver to places on Howe Sound and back again. Its capacity was about one hundred passengers. That day, uncharacteristically, some fifty were Japanese. Ours were to be one-way rides.

I reluctantly joined the departing group and walked up the narrow gangplank. My arms felt the strain of my bags, heavy though they contained but the barest necessities. I felt the vibration as the engine started up. A warning whistle sounded.

> Against such a thing as tears
> Resolved,
> When taking leave of home.
> Yet at that departure whistle,
> My eyes fill.

Facing the docks, I smiled bravely and waved. The din grew louder as the ferry started to move. There were shouted messages, goodbyes and encouragements. Some shouted, 'Take care!' some, 'Sayonara!' One clear voice shouted, 'Banzai!' My wife had some last-minute words for me, but her voice was drowned out in the tumult. I nodded anyway, continuing to wave.

'When will I see my family again?' As there was no way
for me to know, I fought to push the thought from my mind.
And because of this greater concern, I had no time to indulge
the keen homesickness I already felt for my Woodfibre.

My wife's white handkerchief fluttered, one among hundreds of multicoloured handkerchieves and scarves visible on
the dockside. And my little daughter's bright pink-clad form
steadily receded in the distance. This was her first significant
parting from her father. The disheartened sloping of her shoulders revealed her loneliness, a child's loneliness. The image
remains vivid in my memory.

It seemed strange that this day was like any other. The sun
was descending in the western sky, as if nothing unusual were
happening. A strong smell of the sea hung on the breeze.

> After parting,
> In this dimly lit
> Night ferry,
> Leaning against the windowsill,
> Alone, in thought.

Much later, when I chanced to notice, we had already
passed Bowen Island. Its lighthouse was visible on the right-
hand side. Beyond it, in the evening mist, three small patrol
boats, with uniformed figures on deck, materialized as if from
nowhere. They were a common feature of the coastal waters,
but for my consciousness, lately stirred by the evacuation, they
held a new significance. I realized with a shock that war was
indeed upon us.

From the ferry window I could now make out the twinkling
lights of Vancouver. I sank into a bottomless uncertainty.
Some time later, I became conscious of the ferry's having
docked.

To Vancouver and on to Yellowhead road camp

AS SOON AS we Woodfibre evacuees had got
off the ferry at Vancouver, we were loaded onto two waiting
trucks and taken to the assembly centre at Hastings Park Exhibition Grounds. There our nostrils were immediately offended
by a strong stench of cows and horses. We soon realized why,
as we were promptly herded into the building normally used to
house livestock exhibited at the annual Pacific National Exhibition. It was already more than half filled with evacuees from
other places, though this was just the first day of entry into the
centre. The bare concrete floors were lined with row upon row
of beds of straw-filled mattresses. To one side was a hill of bag-
gage that had been piled carelessly high. The air was thick
with tobacco smoke. I started to make up my bed but was
overcome by nausea. I quickly escaped into the outside air.

On that first night I had not a moment of sleep. I took out a
photograph of my wife and our child. In the dim light I could
barely make out the two faces that were so much a part of my
existence. Tears welled up. Still, washed by many heartening
recollections, I fought to reclaim my courage. I prayed that no
matter what difficulties blocked our way, my wife, our
daughter, and I would be reunited once again in good health.

The latter part of March is, in Vancouver, a time of spring warmth. The sun beams strongly upon the earth. The trees are starting to bud. But inside our temporary quarters we were to remain untouched by spring. For us, it lacked its customary rejuvenating power. We were set apart, wrapped in uncertainty and irritability.

During the stay in the Livestock Building I made an effort to spend the daylight hours outdoors. When dusk descended, I had no choice but to return to the dull grey of the concrete floors and the stale atmosphere of tobacco smoke and manure. At night I tunnelled into the bedclothes for some escape. But there, tortured by one disquieting thought after another, my mind would become increasingly awake.

Those around me, sharing my fate, must have felt as I did. Every face bore silent witness to repressed dissatisfaction and complaint. New groups of evacuees were daily crowded into the building.

> Reek of manure,
> Stench of livestock,
> And we are herded,
> Milling –
> Jumble of the battlefield.

My only wish was to be liberated, even one day sooner, from this stifling environment. Together with upwards of a thousand other Issei men who had been gathered from the coastal area of British Columbia, I thus passed five days in a state of restless inactivity.

Then on March 21, at 7:15 pm, a special CNR train pulled into a siding not far from Hastings Park. It was to deliver men to a string of road camps in the Rockies, along the Alberta border. We Woodfibre men were in a group of one hundred and fifty destined for Yellowhead, nearly five hundred miles from Vancouver. Having paced in the confines of Hastings Park, I was glad of the release, regardless of where we were to be taken. If there were to be new problems in the future, they would be faced then.

Inside the train, heedless of the night's growing old, men with nerves pulled taut by the unjust evacuation had no thought of sleeping. Some noisily vented their views. Others got drunk and then started either boisterously singing or bickering, sometimes to the point of fisticuffs. There must have been guards, but no one seemed to care. The uproar called to mind a disturbed wasps' nest. I marvelled how, in the circumstances created by war, people threw off their inhibitions and were suddenly thus transformed.

Meanwhile the train moved unrelentingly towards its destination, cutting through the mysterious darkness of night in unknown territory. Occasionally it let out puffs of steam as it strained at curves and panted up inclines. Finally, after a day, another night, and another morning of brawling, it released its strange cargo.

There was not a human habitation in sight, there at the base of the tall mountains. This was at the place called Yellowhead, BC, some thirty-eight hundred feet above sea level and not far from Jasper, Alberta. The bright noonday sun shed great warmth even though the ground was covered with snow. I followed along after the others with my khaki-coloured duffel bag slung across my back and a small old suitcase in my free hand. In the deep snow, a string of twelve freight cars (on loan from the CNR) awaited us as our home.

> Viewed upon arrival,
> More so than rumoured,
> Rockies
> Steep snow peaks
> Rise sharply above the roofs.

Stepping up to look into the car to which eleven others and I were assigned, I quickly took in the scanty features of the accommodation. Six bunk beds were strung like shelves against the walls. In the centre of the car stood only a coal-burning, potbellied stove. In the weeks to come, some of the men would build a small rough table and benches to occupy the space to one side of it. There, by the light of a kerosene lamp, we would read, write letters, or play shogi, go, or cards. But this was all in the future. That day, though tired from the train trip, I immediately unpacked my bags and made my bed so as to have somewhere to stretch my cramped legs. Then, at last, I got a much needed rest. The rest of that first day passed uneventfully as we concentrated on making ourselves as comfortable as possible in our new quarters. On my first night in the Rockies I was uneasy with concern for my family and with wondering what the next day's work would be like.

The next morning, at around seven, I stepped from the box-car into a dark outdoors. It seemed that dawn came late in the tall mountains. I felt the morning chill and sensed that it was colder there than in Vancouver. But I was gratified by the freshness after the stale air of the train trip and of Hastings Park. I proceeded to one of the central cars in the string. It was being used as the dining area. An earlier shift of men who had already eaten breakfast was on its way out as our shift went in, making the area lively with comings and goings. Inside the car a warm homely scene greeted my eyes. At the kitchen end, a number of white cooks with red faces were busy preparing large quantities of steaming hot food. The remaining space was taken up by long tables with benches on either side. On these tables were several large platters piled high with hot cakes. These gave off a delicious aroma, which filled the car and gave me an appetite. There was lots of butter and syrup. Large dishes full of boiled eggs also stood ready. And there was plenty of milk and tea. Everyone might eat as much as he liked. The excellent fare of that first morning did much to soothe the irritability of the newly interned. Indeed, the good food with which we were provided throughout our stay at road camp did much psychologically to alleviate the emotional hardship of the time.

At around eight, with an axe slung over my shoulder, I started out with my fellow workers and followed our white foreman through the lightly falling snow. We were headed for the bush. The path we followed, though not dangerously narrow, was along a ledge that dropped off sharply on one side. Often there were to be a dozen men to a work crew, as there were that morning. The size of the group varied depending on the nature of the work.

The work crews, we discovered, were to be engaged in two projects. The main project, in which I was to be involved, was to clear for use as a road what used to be the old railroad. The new railroad now ran roughly alongside it in a winding course through the valleys between the mountains. The old tracks had become overgrown and littered with boulders that had fallen with the snow down the mountainside.

The secondary project was to set up a tent camp, so that the CNR freight cars could be returned. One work crew was to clear enough of the bush of a relatively level section of the valley. Meanwhile other crews were to work up on the wooded slopes, selecting and felling trees of a uniform size, for logs to be laid down as foundations for the tenthouses. Others were to manage horses in harness, to bring these logs down to the camp area. Still others were to do the carpentry involved in erecting the huge tenthouses.

We had been moved to Yellowhead just so that we would be out of the one-hundred-mile 'protected zone'; now we were to be put to work in what was essentially a make-work program. After only a few miles of road had been cleared, and even before completion of the tent camp, half of us were to be moved away from Yellowhead road camp. This was to happen when we had been there for less than a month.

But to return to that first morning – there I was out in the bush in below-freezing temperature. Unaccustomed to the cold, I felt it keenly. It was as though pins were being thrust into my ears. My fingers grasping the axe grew numb. Luckily we could make a bonfire of the trees we cut down and the undergrowth we cleared. When I was thus about to set fire to a pile I had prepared, I saw a curious sight. A multitude of large reddish-brown ants was scurrying about frenetically. Wondering what they were doing exposed to the cold of March, I knelt down for a closer look. It appeared that they had been dislodged from their home in some rotting wood that I had just thrown onto the pile. Feeling pity at the prospect of their being burned, I scooped them up by handfuls in my gloved hands and released them in an uncleared area.

As I took pleasure in tending the fire, the noisy crackling, popping, hissing of the green wood burning gave rise to child-hood memories and accompanying nostalgia. I remembered how, as a boy in Japan, I had buried sweet potatoes deep into the hot cinders, then had waited with keen anticipation for the delicious treat. In turn I added to the fire pine, spruce, fir, birch, aspen, and other woods. My nostrils tingled from the raw pungent smells given off by the burning conifers. I watched with boyish delight as the thick white smoke dispersed until I could see the bright blue-green and red-orange of the flames. Well warmed by the fire, and having digested a sandwich lunch, I worked to gather more wood for the fire. Pausing for a moment, I gazed off into the distance where I could make out a sunlit lake. It was then that I had my first view of moose. Two were on the shore, their huge heads lowered to drink. I was surprised at their great size, even at that distance.

Our working conditions were good. There was no time pressure. Each man worked as he saw his fellows working, taking short breaks as he found them necessary. In the homogeneous group our work crew was, all men from Woodfibre, all about the same age, all working-class, and all sharing the same fate, there was a great sense of fellowship, and much talking as we went about our jobs.

In these conditions, in this inspiring rugged setting, I worked contentedly. The afternoon sky was clear; but, from the clouds that hung about the mountain peaks, a fine rain fell and gently washed my face, flushed from labour beneath a bright sun. Later, when as was characteristic of such an area, the sun dropped early behind the mountains to the west, the downwinds of the Rockies whistled from the peaks, more viciously than rumoured, and the temperature dropped suddenly. Soon thereafter we returned to our boxcar camp and enjoyed a satisfying meal of beef stew, bread and butter, and tea.

In the evening I stepped outdoors to gaze at the pale crescent moon at the edge of the mountains. And I thought of how that same moon shone on my wife and our child, on the other side. When I went to bed, the cold and the loneliness pressed in and seemed to freeze even my visions of Woodfibre.

Life at Yellowhead

I HAD NOW BEEN at Yellowhead road camp
for two weeks. It being a weekday morning, I again set out
early for work in the cold outdoors. I looked at the peak to the
north with particular interest, having been told that it was
Mount Robson, the highest peak in the Canadian Rockies.
With uplifted spirits I took a deep draught of the cold invigo-
rating air and swung my axe with zest. The mountains returned an echo that rebounded across the valley for some
minutes, until I sensed through it their majesty filling me. In
the bush close behind I heard a rustling noise, turned, and was
startled by the sight of a large black bear foraging for food. Our
eyes met briefly before it apparently decided we humans were
too close by, and ambled away.

Looking back to those days, I am struck by how conducive
conditions were to my resuming the writing of tanka verse.
The practice began simply enough. Having made tentative
physical and emotional adjustments to being at Yellowhead, I
found that I had spare time and energy after the day's work
was done. And I was not one who enjoyed games. But the
many novel features of my surroundings, seen en route to and

from work each day, inspired me, and I became excited about the challenge of creating beautiful poems to reflect them. Onto this endeavour I then focused my energy.

My practice of tanka composition was confirmed as part of meeting a still greater need. The near-traumatic separation from my family had meant the sudden removal of important emotional supports, and had necessitated a change in the way I coped with the daily vicissitudes of life. At this time of vulnerability my spirit was malleable, susceptible to any compelling power. As it happened, nature was to be that power. The tanka would serve both to order my perception of nature and to give expression to that perception.

But let me return to that day in the bush. It was now late afternoon. Just this side of the mountain range to the east was an exposed incline, already showing sparse vegetation through the snow. My attention was captured by five moose grazing there. Wondering if there might not be other animals to see, I slowly scanned the area. Suddenly bright light broke through the clouds. I lost sight of the moose. To my surprise I found that I was witnessing the forming of a rainbow. It grew and grew until it had erected a great arch to span the crests of seven mountains. The splendour spread out before my eyes permeated my being until I felt first filled to satiety, then strangely subdued. It was as though my personality had been engulfed by something much larger. I was left numbed.

When after a time I suddenly came to myself, the rainbow had vanished. Looking around quickly to the west, I saw that the sun had started to descend towards the edge of the mountains. As it did so the glaciers on the peaks changed colour moment by moment – now pink, then mauve, then deep purple, and finally grey. There, in that vast classroom of nature, the compelling power sought by my spirit had been found. I had been writing tanka for years, but here my spirit first learned the excitement of the poetic urge.

With the approach of twilight the moose withdrew to the forest for the night, presenting as they went a peaceful sunset scene, idyllic enough to be a landscape mural. At the same time a myriad of tiny mountain sparrows settled into the underbrush behind me. The enveloping hush of the mountains was so deep that I could hear a faint rustling of dead leaves disturbed by tiny wings.

The inclines were now in darkness, but the peaks still received light from the sun. This evening light faded gradually until the peaks too at last disappeared. A thick blanket of blackness descended whilst the winds began to blow down off the mountains and bit into my flesh. Even early April was, in the Rockies, as cold as had been rumoured in Woodfibre. And the heavy load of sadness that I carried in my heart made me more susceptible to the cold.

Since my arrival in Canada I had kept a diary. Between the start of the Japan-U.S. conflict in late 1941 and the evacuation from Woodfibre on March 16, I had looked through the accumulated diaries of over twenty years. Because a return to Woodfibre had seemed doubtful even then, I had selected three of my most treasured diaries, those containing some earlier attempts at tanka. These I had placed at the bottom of my suitcase along with a Bible, which was the only book I packed.

In the Rockies, too, I kept a diary. Interspersed amongst the entries were the tanka tinged with loneliness that I composed in profusion. Now, looking back over my life, I see that never was there a time at which I kept my diary as religiously as in those days. The Issei then was haunted by anxiety about his future, contingent upon the duration of the war and its outcome. Even the immediate future was unknowable. The uncertainty was such as to force thoughts even to the point of pondering death. Death meant non-existence. I thought that unless I left behind something, if only a diary, one man's life on this earth might pass without having left a trace.

Since I had no intimate friend to whom I could open my heart, I generally went early to bed. In the early evening I read what books I could borrow from the others, then wrote my diary entry and some tanka. At those times when my loneliness was particularly acute, I went to stand under the night sky. And it seemed to rain something sympathetic upon me. As I gently closed my eyes to feel the moonlight on their lids, the present misery seemed to dissipate. Then was I back in Woodfibre, my wife and our child and I sitting around the table at an enjoyable evening meal ... But this was an insubstantial dream.

On that night at the end of my second week at Yellowhead, as I thus stood alone and empty, there came from somewhere the low tones of a lone *shakuhachi* (bamboo flute). The delicate sound seemed out of place in that austere environment, and so I listened all the more attentively. As each poignant note sounded I had flashes of a now-distant life in Japan, and was steadily brought to feel as a traveller far from home.

Before dawn the next morning a heavy rain pelted against the freight car. By the time we got up the rain had subsided. With the coming of daylight, a clear sky spread over the Rockies. The mountains to the east loomed large on the horizon. As axe in tow I headed out to work, I disturbed the rain caught in the branches; it fell about my head and shoulders.

I spent the morning and the early afternoon again swinging my axe in the valley coppice. Around mid-afternoon, just as I was beginning to feel fatigued, a heavy rain beat down, making us scatter for shelter. As the atmosphere became a heavy whiteness, the mountains changed to looming spectres. To one side of us the creek, its water muddied, flowed more noisily. From the distant mountains came the muffled yet disquieting howl of a coyote. Our foreman decided that we would stop work early. As happy as schoolboys let out of class early, we hurried back to our boxcar camp. And just a thunderstorm, the rain stopped soon after we arrived there.

The spring night sky looked as if it had been washed by the
heavy rains of the day. The clouds had all dissipated, leaving it
completely clear. There at that distant road camp I looked
up to moonlit peaks to the west and sent my thoughts over
them, to my family on the other side.

The temperature that night, as on other nights, was down
about ten degrees below zero. But once we had shut the door
of the boxcar we seemed to have shut out the coldness for the
night. Having returned from supper in the dining car, all
twelve of us gathered around the potbellied stove. I enjoyed
the lively talk on many subjects that ensued. Again wild conjectures ran rife in the absence of any real news. And of course
we recounted at length our various pasts. Nevertheless, as I
looked around me, I could not help but think what a sorry
scene we comprised. Here were men who had fallen from a
better state and had lost some of their human dignity by the
fall.

Soon after our arrival at Yellowhead the go- and shogi-
playing and the gambling at cards had started. The latter was
especially popular; every evening some four or five gathered
around the small table beside the stove and commenced play.
Some of the men were from neighbouring cars. It seemed that
the same young players always lost. Not being a card player
myself, I often wondered why they had to play for money.
Crowded twelve to a car as we were, with our liberty gone and
without hope for the future, it was inevitable that we would
come to consider only the present and seek only what was
immediately gratifying. Yet the sight of still-impressionable
youths, with spirits decaying for lack of stimulation and hope,
had to be lamented.

One Sunday, at the urging of a friend, I joined him and four
others for an outing to collect unusual rocks and perhaps to
chance upon a pair of antlers. That afternoon we saw the
watershed of the Rockies. The site we visited was located on
the border between British Columbia and Alberta. I pondered

upon the inscription in the stone. The clear water that oozes out little by little from between the stones high in the mountains forms a tiny flow, which, as it drops to ever lower levels, whispering over small stones, gains always in size and momentum. Eventually the flow reaches the watershed site where it divides into two streams. One branch flows eastward to empty at last into Hudson Bay; the other branch flows westward to its release into the Pacific. Just a short day later these waters, now in something like a husband-and-wife relationship, would be separated by a thousand miles. The plight of the waters struck a note of recognition in me. I stared and stared at the spot where the one flow divided. Quiet reverie set in.

> Watershed's
> Whispering waters
> Part and flow.
> Separation anxiety
> Revives.

To Descoigne road camp

DURING my third week at Yellowhead I was asked to move to Descoigne road camp, just a few miles away in the direction of Jasper. Apparently Yellowhead had more workers than were needed while Descoigne was shorthanded. My immediate reaction was negative: I wanted to remain in the place whose familiarity now afforded some security. But I also had a vague expectation that a change of surroundings would supply new objects for my curiosity and thus would stimulate fresh thought. Accordingly I joined a group of some seventy-five men, about half the work force of Yellowhead, who on April 15 moved to Descoigne, just beyond the next ridge.

Upon arriving I saw to my great delight that this camp had a feature not found at Yellowhead. Parallel to the now familiar string of boxcars ran a thirty-foot-wide river! The crystal-clear water flowed slowly, as though tired from thousands of years of following that old course.

On the first evening I was treated to the sight of six beavers swimming silently up the river from far downstream. They disappeared near a secluded stretch of the bank, dense with pussy-willow bushes, near which a large mound of earth and branches was visible above the surface of the water.

> A beaver's cry
> At twilight.
> A flower opens –
> The evening primrose –
> On the river bank.

In the weeks to come I was to see many black bears, white-tail deer, moose, elk, and coyotes. These were just some of the animals in which this wilderness area abounded. I learned that the entire district, encompassing Yellowhead too, was part of the famous Jasper National Park, where hunting was prohibited and the animals were quite used to humans.

The hardy pussy-willow, which starts to bud on the river banks in the yet-cold blustery winds, is an early herald of spring. The catkins had appeared, and from beneath the bushes I heard for the first time that year a noisy chorus of croaking frogs. I could picture their throats rhythmically swelling and contracting. I became almost hypnotized by the sound, and my thoughts went back to the carefree springtimes of my youth in rural Japan. The alluring notes of the *shakuhachi* came to draw me gently back to human society. Now much desiring to spend an evening in good company, I sought out the others.

> Spring snows –
> Smell of melting rising –
> Melting down.
> Night fog thickens noiselessly
> And envelops our boxcar home.

The setting of my second road-camp home was quite different from that of my first, though both were located in

Bear cubs visited the road camp at Descoigne

Work crew on Descoigne bridge: Takeo is the second from left in the back row

Unloading coal at Descoigne Road Camp: boxcars were the evacuees' homes

valleys about an eighth of a mile wide. The valley at Yellow-head had seemed narrow, because of the extreme ruggedness of the heavily forested heights that encroached on it from both sides. The valley at Descoigne seemed more open. It was much flatter and looked as if it had experienced much flooding; the vegetation of the valley itself was sparser, and the slopes that flanked it were balding.

The CNR line ran along one side of the river, behind our boxcar camp. Across the valley, on the other side of the river, old railroad tracks ran along the facing range of hills. As at Yellowhead, work crews were set to pulling up whatever had overgrown the tracks, clearing away large boulders, and shovelling the debris in order to level out sections for use as a roadway.

Shortly after our arrival at Descoigne, we built a bridge across the river. We took about forty twenty-foot logs to the selected spot, where the water was only about five feet deep. We laid them side by side, alternating them so that they lay thicker end beside thinner end; the spaces between the logs we packed with stones and dirt. The completed bridge was secure enough to support a two-horse wagon and its load. As we lived across the river from the road-work site, we used the bridge to get to work. The river was not, however, very deep at any point. The clearness of the water revealed the riverbed beneath. Because the bottom was clay rather than rock, a rainfall did make the water muddy. But fed by fresh mountain streams, the river was generally clean.

One day as I was busy shovelling debris from the old railroad, I saw in the river two bears, skilfully catching fish and offering them to two waiting cubs. Now, the black bear was especially bold. A number often visited the camp to go through the garbage, and the cooks sometimes saved us scraps of meat to feed them. The bears even learned to take pieces from the palms of the outstretched hands of the two or three men who were foolhardy enough to let them come so near. The bears generally gobbled the meat ravenously, but sometimes, probably when they were full, they held the pieces in their mouths and ambled off into the woods.

On that day, as I looked upon the river feeding scene, I felt a warm smile spreading over my face. I began to recall the famous legend of one Kintaro of Ashigara Mountain. When I was a child my grandfather had often delighted me with the tale. I soon found myself singing the little lyric that accompanied the story. Before long I felt that I had recaptured the spirit of the innocent boy I had once been. I tried to retrieve the tale from my memory ...

This tale took place a long long time ago. Deep in the wilderness of Ashigara Mountain lived a very healthy and strong boy named Kintaro. He lived with his mother, just the two of them. Because in the wilderness there were no toys, he amused himself all day long by wielding his axe to fell trees.

One day a big black bear appeared and said, 'It's you, is it, who's been destroying my forest?' and leapt at Kintaro. Kintaro threw down his axe, grappled with the bear, and soon managed to throw him.

Now in the woods it is the strongest who becomes lord. The defeated bear had to become Kintaro's vassal. Seeing this, all the animals who had been the bear's vassals came out of the woods in droves and acknowledged Kintaro as their lord.

In the carefree days that followed, Kintaro often returned to that spot in the woods and called, 'Hallo, come on out!' In answer to his voice the bear, the deer, the fox, the raccoon, the rabbit, and others came bounding out. Then they all sported about the woods together as friends. Sometimes Kintaro practised riding on the bear's back, as on a horse's.

Often they wrestled in some grassy sunlit clearing. On one occasion Kintaro said, 'Today, all of you come at me together!' The bear, the deer, the monkey, the rabbit, all the animals, right down even to the small chipmunk, fell at once upon him. But one by one they were all thrown off and stood defeated.

Having played hard, all were hungry. The good-hearted Kintaro now shared with his friends the rice-balls his mother had made him. 'Oh, delicious!' they all piped in unison.

When the animals were escorting Kintaro home, the group took a different route from the usual one and came to a gorge. Kintaro pulled down a thick cedar to span the gorge as a bridge. All trooped across.

As it happened, Kintaro's uncle was observing the scene from a distance. He hurried over to say, 'What splendid strength you have! You should become a samurai.' It was thus decided that Kintaro would go to the capital of Kyoto, where he was later to become a famous samurai. With a cheerful 'I'm off!' Kintaro departed.

The great strength of young Kintaro, to whose power anything is possible, makes him the child's hero. But the tale of Kintaro can be heartening to persons of any age, provided they can still see with the eyes of a child, and know with the heart of one.

Life at Descoigne

FOR SOME WEEKS, then, at Descoigne road camp work crews had been hurrying to complete the tenthouses. On May 15, a month after the arrival of our group from Yellowhead, we were able to move into them. We must have composed quite a scene when, like a troupe of snails, with our belongings on our backs, we slowly made our way in a long straggling line, winding in and out among the trees from the boxcars to our new homes. 'What a strange fate is ours,' I thought to myself.

Five brand new orange canvas tenthouses lined up on the green turf, a splash of colour against the background of the many greens of the spring trees.

Inside, these new quarters were set up much like our old. Visible from the one entrance were fifteen bunk beds lining three walls; in the centre space were the stove, the table, and the benches. The spaciousness of these forty-foot by thirty-foot tenthouses at first seemed quite a blessing. Now, however, thirty, rather than the twelve of the boxcar, were housed under one roof. During the day, when all were out at work, the tenthouse was in silence. In the evening it came alive with the larger group, all engaged in playing go or cards or in group singing. As over half of the camp of one hundred and fifty were from places other than Yellowhead, the conversation was again lively with the exchanging of experiences.

Because the tenthouse was one large room with no partitions, even the beds had no privacy. Like it or not, we were all one big family. If the noisy partying continued late into the night, few could sleep. But goodwill prevailed among those sharing a common fate and soothed any irritation. With familiarity, I found that I did not mind tenthouse living, which I was then experiencing for the first time in my life.

At dawn, the tunes of birds of many varieties would come to me while I was still lying in the darkness. Still drowsy, I could sink into the bedclothes for those luxurious few minutes more, then be gently and gradually brought to waking. From a distance, the murmur of a small creek trickling over pebbles was faintly audible.

Just a step outside the tenthouse, blinking from the sudden light, I would take a deep breath of the exhilarating air and come awake. I was heartened by the sight of Mount Robson, visible from there as from Yellowhead. Just steps from the entrance, I would kneel to rinse my face in the pure waters of the mountain creek.

> From high in the Rockies,
> Overflowing boulders,
> Gushing downward,
> Clear cold water
> My life sustains.

One morning, a flock of mountain sparrows settled into the trees across the creek. Unable to resist the sudden urge, I clapped together my wet hands, making a smacking sound. The birds took flight, all at one instant, scolding me for the intrusion.

As I took a short stroll, the sun would show its face in the pink eastern sky. A light breeze often would stir the young leaves of the poplars and set them shimmering silver-white in the early sunlight. One day my customary morning walk was interrupted by the whistle of a CNR locomotive emerging from a tunnel in the mountainside. Emitting clouds of grey smoke, the train passed slowly through the valley. Though not an uncommon sight it caught my attention, partly because trains seemed incongruous with the peaceful seclusion of those mountains. As if with the intently curious eyes of a child, I happily followed the train until it disappeared around a bend in the tracks. I heard the whistle sound again, and this time it was like a call to work, for the rest of the camp soon began to stir and I was launched into the day's activities. I headed to the kitchen for breakfast, marvelling that some Department of National Defence officials could fear that the likes of us road camp workers might sabotage the railways.

Mid-May was also when, for the first time since I had begun work in the road camps, I received some pay. I opened the envelope expectantly, thinking that, though the wage scale was low, seven weeks' accumulation would be substantial. To my surprise, there was only $4.75! I stared at the money, puzzled at the calculation that could have produced so meagre an amount. I made inquiries. I learned that for one thing, due to bureaucratic delays, this pay was for one month, not seven weeks. The calculations were as follows. After deduction for room and board, the basic pay was $20 per month. From this, $15 went to the support of my family. The final 25-cent deduction was, if I recall correctly, for workmen's compensation. That left me with $4.75. 'What a miserable sum!' I could not help thinking.

What made me especially happy at Descoigne camp was that I was able to bathe in a Japanese bath, for the first time in the two months since I had left Woodfibre. Back on the coast I had become accustomed to bathing in one nightly. But thus far in the life of the road camp, even showers had not been possible. Instead we had heated basins of water on the stove in our tenthouse, then had rushed out back with them to sponge-bathe in privacy. This had made for a short scrub as the cold quickly chased us indoors again. Now the newly built Japanese bath was a popular spot indeed. Though makeshift, it served its purpose well. A roughly constructed shed housed a wooden boxlike tub, five feet by five feet and about three feet deep. This was filled almost to the top with water that was continuously warmed by a wood fire burning underneath the brickwork base. On one side a waterspout from outdoors reached in past the rim of the tub. It was used to fill the tub initially and then to add cold water to adjust the temperature. On the wooden platform outside the tub, four or five men would be busy soaping themselves and then rinsing off in preparation for getting into the tub. Meanwhile two or three others would already be in it, squatting on their haunches so that the water came up to their necks, thoroughly warming them and relieving muscles sore from the day's work. How happy we all were with this last vestige of a lifestyle now far behind us in both time and space.

On Sunday mornings we indulged in the luxury of lying late in bed. Thus it was late morning when my young friend and I took a long walk along the river bank one Sunday. The sky above was clear, but up the river a distance the waters were still misted over. Out of this fog came the occasional faint cry of a beaver. Otherwise, as there was no work in progress that day, a deep hush covered all.

Fuku walked behind me. I turned around when he suddenly burst into lively song. Looking into his face, I saw a sunny expression and eyes twinkling mischievously. The song was a familiar Japanese tune. The lyrics tell of a young university student playing a *shakuhachi*, not because he enjoys it, but because he must. Already given up by his parents as a ne'er-do-well, he has now, besides, failed his examinations. He has no choice but to go from door to door, disguised by a large hood over his head, playing the *shakuhachi* and begging for his livelihood. Though the lyrics were not happy, the liveliness of the tune and Fuku's fine singing irresistibly drew me into participation.

And so it often was with my friend. It was he who at Yellowhead had urged me to join the outing to the watershed. He possessed an infectious enthusiasm. He was lighthearted, and I remember him as constantly amusing me with witty jokes. He was a handsome and spirited young man, and one of those who skilfully managed the horses that towed logs down the mountainside. An Issei of thirty years, he had arrived at Woodfibre ten years earlier. We had known each other there, but it had taken the altered circumstances of wartime to turn us into friends.

Having eaten our sandwiches and washed them down with cool draughts from the river, we continued for some distance along the bank. We picked horsetails and watercress, to be enjoyed that evening as a special treat. While we were thus absorbed, a small plane, perhaps on patrol, flew by high overhead. The somehow ominous sound of its engine made me look up, my nerves suddenly a little on edge. How near the surface of my consciousness lay constant awareness of our uncertain lot, even there in that deceptively peaceful existence.

Back from the river, on the grassy hillside, dandelions bloomed like stars. Growing at our feet were the wild roses of Alberta. I picked some, then added daisies, buttercups, violets, and other flowers from the colourful abundance around us. Even today, several decades later, the names of these pretty flowers remind me of the peace of those days at Descoigne road camp, and comfort me as I cope with the restless big-city life of my postwar years.

While spring slowly passed through the Rockies, I delighted in the beauty of the wild flowers. Often I lay down amongst them on the grassy slopes and wrote long letters to my wife and daughter. Each time I included poems composed on the spot. Until late May, my family was still in Woodfibre. In those days Yukie put in her letters to me pretty pressed sweet peas, snapdragons, and pansies from the garden of our home. Sometimes there were several poems. One told of the Japanese woman in Canada, now alone coping with the rearing of a child; she was to be brave in the face of adversity, taking as her model the renowned stouthearted Japanese woman of the Meiji era. Another poem told of the lively children's songs Yukie sang to Toshimi, to divert her when she persisted in questions about her father.

In early July, when I had been at Descoigne for two and a half months, two officials from the BC Security Commission came one day with an announcement. We all gathered in the camp kitchen, wondering what was to happen next. Great were our relief and joy at the news. Soon Descoigne camp would be closed, and all men with families would be sent to the ghost towns in the interior to which their families had been evacuated. With this to look forward to, we were to continue to work obediently until the happy day came. Upon hearing these words I felt a burden lift from my heart. With new hope, I told myself to endure just a little while longer. Soon I was to be on my way to Greenwood, there to be reunited with Yukie and Toshimi.

To Slocan instead of Greenwood

ON JULY 27, less than a month after the visit of the Security Commission representatives, Descoigne road camp was closed. We were all to proceed initially to Hope, BC. How cheerful was everyone's expression that morning! You see, we all expected that from Hope each man would be sent to the ghost town in which his family now lived.

Looking down the tracks in the direction the train would be taking us, I saw a perfectly clear sky and felt that this boded good. Moreover we were going back towards the coast, towards civilization. When the train arrived, I saw that quite a crowd had accumulated on it, since all the road camps in the area were being closed. We eagerly climbed aboard.

My joy at departure was not wholly unqualified. Descoigne had been my home, after all, for upwards of three months. I paused to thank quietly the Rocky Mountains whose majestic beauty had now encouraged me, now consoled me, in my daily existence. I said goodbye as to a friend. I wondered when I would again see the Rockies. As the train pulled away, the scenery dropped off behind.

Finally filled to capacity, the train arrived at Hope in the early afternoon of the next day. There we were detained for about five hours while we were individually interviewed by Japanese-speaking Nisei working with the Security Commission for the orderly relocation of evacuees. The object was to ascertain the ghost town in which each man's family had been relocated. Groups were formed accordingly, destined for such places as Slocan, Sandon, New Denver, Kaslo, Greenwood, and Tashme.

I was one of seven men whose families were in Greenwood. When my turn to be interviewed came, I naturally asked to be sent there. The interviewer said, 'Since they are short of workers at Slocan, we would like you to go there to work.' What a blow! I could not believe I had heard him correctly. My throat constricted and went dry. In the month since learning that we were to leave Descoigne, I had never once considered the possibility that I would be sent anywhere other than Greenwood.

Because I was caught so unawares, my reaction was not carefully considered. But struggling to keep my tone even, I addressed the interviewer thus: 'When I was at the road camp, two Security Commission officials came and made a promise. What you are now saying does not concur with it. I demand that the promise be kept.' I pursued my point. I stated that I wished to be sent to Greenwood, where my family was, just as others were being sent to the ghost towns where their families were. The interviewer was equally persistent. He explained that at Slocan workers were needed to complete housing for more evacuees from Vancouver, for families that now were being moved intact. When I remained unmoved, he abruptly ended the interview by firmly stating that I should go to Slocan. He added, however, that it was not far from Greenwood, and that I could take the matter up with the Security

Commission centre to be found there. We seven realized that
nothing could be accomplished in the confusion of the five
hundred-odd being interviewed at Hope, and decided to do as we
were advised. We joined forces with eight men who were in the
same position, only their families were in Kaslo, and determined
to win our way with the Security Commission at Slocan.

After supper in a local restaurant we left Hope that same
evening, Slocan-bound. The next day, July 29, at around four
in the afternoon, the train stopped for two minutes at Greenwood. At least one of the other six had had the presence of
mind to telegraph ahead. For there at the station were our
families! After a separation of over four months, the sight of
the healthy faces of Yukie and Toshimi made my heart dance
with joy. Yet there was hardly time to clutch each other's
hands and converse in two hurried minutes. With extreme
reluctance I reboarded the train, which departed without
delay. My heart dragged behind in Greenwood, though I was
carried on towards Slocan.

> Child by the hand,
> In midsummer swelter,
> Railroad station scene.
> Come to greet me,
> Narrow eyebrows of my wife.

The sun dropped behind the distant mountains. Soon the
light from the train windows illuminated only the brush that
approached the tracks from either side. Beyond, all lay in mysterious darkness. That night the train now and then made
stops at small stations. It was a very slow ride. With dawn I
saw pastures spread out on either side of the tracks. Such areas
were not to be found in the small island country of Japan; I
had hitherto known them only in pictures. On a gentle slope

of land I saw a flock of sheep being taken out to graze. The train seemed to be moving deeper into the mountains into a sparsely settled area. The homesteads became fewer. Toward sunset, hill country was visible to the right and to the left. And we must have been moving up an incline: I felt the intermittent vibrations as the engineer accelerated to help us up the grade.

We pulled into the station at Nelson. After months of Western-style food, we heartily enjoyed an evening meal at the local Chinese restaurant to which we had been directed. Even this occasion, however, was not without incident. We fifteen, straggling behind the main group of others from the train for Slocan, left the restaurant after telling the proprietor that the Security Commission would pick up the tab. This was not an unreasonable assumption, as such had been the case at the Hope restaurant, and the train meals had all been provided. The proprietor looked quite skeptical, but could not detain us. We had settled ourselves back on the train when, through the windows, we saw him running towards us, waving his arms and calling out in a loud voice. He had learned that we were mistaken and had ourselves to pay for our dinners. Fortunately, we had been told to keep our orders modest. As we reached into our pockets we were annoyed. But we soon realized that the commotion at the train door was not without its humorous side.

We settled down to spend yet another night sleeping seated in the train. The train was motionless, but this proved no advantage. Rather, it was more difficult to sleep without the lulling effect of movement. We were being kept at Nelson so as to arrive at Slocan at the right time: with hundreds of people being moved into the area, some organization was necessary.

In the morning the train crept into a narrow valley. Noon of July 31 found us at Slocan. Likely our manner of approach influenced my first impression of the place, which was that it was much more isolated than I had expected. There I was back in the interior of British Columbia, having travelled over seven hundred miles since leaving Descoigne, yet still not where my family was.

Right on that first afternoon all fifteen of us, the seven who wanted to go to Greenwood plus the eight who wanted to go to Kaslo, sought out the Security Commission centre. There we again dealt with Nisei interviewers to whom we told our story. While still at the road camp, we explained, we had been told what we had taken for a promise, that at its closing we were to be sent to the ghost towns where our families lived. We then told how we had therefore worked patiently for another four weeks, waiting for that day to come. We stated our position: we deplored the breaking of the promise. In reply, we were again told that workers were needed at Slocan.

We knew what we had to do. For four days from August 1 through August 4, we did not work. And three representatives, who were the most vocal members of our group, went to the Security Commission centre to negotiate. But the efforts were to no avail. And they came to a bad end, for the authorities decided to send all fifteen of us to the Immigration Building jail at Vancouver. The worst was now in store for us. To be sent to the Immigration Building jail could mean only one thing. From there, sooner or later, one was sent far east, to the prisoner-of-war camp at Angler, Ontario.

I can't express the anger and chagrin that I felt at that moment on August 4, when I learned of this decision. Perhaps to some we had created a problem where none had existed. To rashly buck the authorities instead of patiently doing a stint at Slocan, and to thus land ourselves in such a predicament, might have appeared quite foolish. But in view of the Security Commission's having broken faith with us, we had acted instinctively.

Not one of us had a quiet mind or heart on the night of
August 4. The persistent chirping of the crickets increased the
atmosphere of sorrow. Then, as if to underscore our wretched
state, fierce thunder and lightning accompanied rain enough to
squash the flimsy two-man tents in which we newcomers
slept. I fell into a state in which it seemed that what was happening to me was all just a bad dream.

The summer night is short and the dawn comes early. The
dawn of August 5 was like any other. But how vastly had my
world changed. In just one day a completely undreamed-of
upheaval had occurred. I was soon to be in jail, a miserable
prisoner. Even in the light of day, my thought could not follow
the reality of what was to be.

After the heavy downpour of the previous night, the sky
was clear. Soon the entire Slocan valley, with its placid lake,
lay open to my view. It was flanked by gentle slopes, grassy
but unforested. Between these nestled the valley, still sleeping
in the morning air. As it grew lighter all about me, I com-
mitted my hopes to the single lingering star visible in the
morning sky.

Before long the August sun beat strongly on the valley that
spread out before me in continuous shades of green. I gazed at
the scene to drink it in, in preparation for my return to a city
environment. Early the next day we were to start off on yet
another five-hundred-mile journey, under Mountie guard, to
the Immigration Building at Vancouver.

To jail
in Vancouver

IT WAS the morning of August 6, and we
fifteen troublemakers were up before daybreak to eat a simple
breakfast. Before we had finished it, two Mounted Policemen
appeared and ordered us into a truck. Unaccustomed to our
new status, we were irritated by their severity. For the first
time in my life, I had a doubly miserable status: I was a
national of a country that was at war with my country of
residence, and I was soon to be a prisoner.

Under the watchful eyes of the Mounties, who followed
close behind in their car, the truck sped through the darkness. It shook us up as it travelled over a rough road along a
narrow mountain ledge. Several times I thought that we would
momentarily drop off a cliff. My whole body shrank with fear.
I was much relieved when we arrived at Nelson in well under
an hour. The train was at the station. We fifteen were put in a
specially designated car. Not for a moment did either of the
Mounties relax his vigilant eyes. The atmosphere was decidedly menacing.

We could not get to Vancouver without passing through
Greenwood, and again the brevity of the joy would make it
painful. I struggled uselessly to calm myself.

This time the train stopped at Greenwood for only one minute. And this time, as a prisoner, I was not allowed to get off. Yukie and Toshimi were there, looking tearful and waving their handkerchieves at me. It all happened so quickly. We shouted messages through the open window. Since it was certain that I would be sent to prison in Ontario, I reasoned that I would not need much money whereas Yukie could well use any amount, having been forced to leave almost everything with the Custodian when she was evacuated from Woodfibre. I therefore wrapped most of the little cash I had in a handkerchief and threw it to her as the train began to pull away. For as long as I could make out the figures of mother and child I continued to wave. Then I slumped down into the seat. Without the energy to look at the changing scenery, I remained in a kind of stupor throughout the night and well into the next day, till I was roused by our arrival at Vancouver.

The Immigration Building was an uninteresting rectangular two-storey structure on the waterfront. To one side were the docks, and to the other the freight station, of the CPR. In the early afternoon we were taken off the train and escorted towards the Immigration Building, where I saw Canadian soldiers for the first time. The shame of the subdued prisoner burned within me when I felt their hard scrutiny. We were promptly assembled in a large room from which we were called out individually, relieved of whatever we had with us, and then led to the jail on the second floor. The jail consisted of one large room with only one small window. Much to my surprise, there were not even cots or benches.

The over thirty Japanese inmates who were already there rejoiced at the arrival of fellows who they of course assumed shared their cause. You see, these inmates were what were known as *gambariya*. They are best described as rebels against the treatment they were receiving in time of war. The Nisei *gambariya* were protesting such unjust treatment of Canadian

citizens as they were experiencing; the Issei *gambariya* firmly
believed in Japan's eventual victory and looked forward to the
Canadian government's enforced compensation to them. These
men had actively sought confinement and looked forward to
the challenge of internment at the Angler prisoner-of-war
camp. The sentiments of us newcomers were quite the opposite: we had absolutely no desire to be imprisoned.

I soon noticed the pallor of those jailed earlier and became
worried. I resolved, however, to cope as best I could with the
miserable lot that I now shared with them. Thick walls closed
us in on all sides. And while the iron bars could not keep out
the sunlight that streamed in through the small window, the
interior was decidedly gloomy. The emotional strain of being
jailed had given me a severe headache. I wrapped myself in the
single blanket that had been issued to me and lay down on the
wooden floor.

I watched the complexions of my companions grow paler by
the day and felt my confidence being gradually undermined.
Indeed, there was precious little to raise my spirits. Neither a
letter from my wife nor even a newspaper reached me. And of
course there had been no communication from my family in
Japan since Pearl Harbor. The outside world was for me
shrouded in complete darkness.

We took turns standing before the window to gaze outside
and breathe deeply of the fresh air. What a luxury, since with
many of us in cramped quarters the air was always stale. We
were confined day and night and not once let out for fresh air
and exercise.

To be able to look up and see even this small square of blue
sky made me happy. And stepping right up to the window, I
had access to a view of sorts. Below me I could see the dozens
of rails of the CPR freight yard. Beyond these were the dirty
back streets of an area of factories. In the distance, just visible,
were some city sidewalks where we occasionally spotted young

women passing by. The inmates seized upon this diversion to
combat boredom. One or two would stand at the window and
describe a passing beauty in vivid terms, teasing the others
who scrambled forward to catch a glimpse. They always got
there too late. Sometimes I would be standing at the window
when a young woman passed by; the sight had its sentimental
appeal. But in those circumstances, with liberty gone and my
predominant mood dejection, it offered little inspiration.

The side of the Immigration Building that protruded over
the water was set high on concrete pillars. On a quiet night I
could hear the waves hitting the rocky shore.

> Faintly plashing,
> Waves hit the shore
> Beneath the floorboards.
> Windowless walls,
> Yet that penetrating sound.

The occasional plaintive cry of a plover sent fleeting sorrow
through me. The peaceful night was disrupted by the banging
of freight cars being linked together on the rails below us. Each
time there was a tremendous crash and a violent vibration.
Our sleep was broken every night.

The boredom of day upon day of inactivity was alleviated
once or twice by the appearance of two or three wives of *gambariya*. Their husbands were either hiding out in Vancouver
resisting relocation, and therefore could not risk appearing
themselves, or had already been sent to Angler. The women
came to encourage their husbands' fellows; they feared that
the inmates might be weakening under confinement. They
waved white handkerchieves to attract our attention and
shouted loudly in unison from a safe distance. The message
was always that the *gambariya* should remain firm. To us
inside, the chant was only faintly audible. But the sight of

the women was heartening, if only because it served to assure us that we were not forsaken by the outside world. Soon the soldiers patrolling the building grounds would spot the women and chase them away. They scattered quickly, but not dejectedly.

Perhaps spurred on by one of these appearances, an especially die-hard *gambariya*, who had once been a Japanese soldier, one day said, 'It will be Japanese-army style in the Angler prisoner-of-war camp. All the inmates will have their hair closely cropped. We must do likewise in preparation for our imprisonment.' He argued that this would stir up the Japanese militaristic spirit. His clamour could not be quelled except by compliance. So each of us, even the one teenager, had his hair cut very short. Imagine our surprise and chagrin when we reached Angler and found that not one of the eight hundred prisoners had a closely cropped head!

On nights when sleep would not come, I invariably went over the failed negotiations at Slocan. Up to that point in my life I had not thought much of the so-called fate of which people often spoke. But in the course of recent events I had learned that in this world fate was indeed at work. I wanted to pursue my thoughts on this and related matters in discussion with some confidant. I had no one, however, with whom I could talk heart-to-heart. Even my young friend Fuku was no longer of our group. He had no family living in a ghost town, so he had quietly gone to Slocan. Past events and current worries crowded into my troubled mind. I was anxious about the safety of my family in Greenwood and of my parents, siblings, and other relatives in Japan, and felt my impotence. I could do nothing for them. I could only sit and hope for the speedy return of peace.

The army was in charge of supplying our meals. The menus were the same each day. Breakfast was two pieces of toast, lunch was a plain dry sandwich, and supper was beef stew and a slice of bread; one cup of tea was served with each meal. The food was unappetizing, yet it did matter that we got so little of it. Perhaps the meagre portions were in consideration of our lack of exercise. Or were they to teach the intransigent a lesson?

After dinner one evening, a large parcel appeared at the jail-room door. Several voices announced its arrival. We who had been lying about on the floor, resting or engaged in conversation, jumped up and gathered around the parcel, smiling in anticipation as several men began to open it. As soon as the seal was broken, a tasty aroma announced what was in store for us – a fine Japanese spread. Soon, like eager children, we were feasting on rice cakes and a fish cake and mixed vegetable dish. You can imagine my delight in what was my first taste of Japanese food since leaving Woodfibre five months earlier. This treat, in such wretched circumstances, brought tears of happiness to my eyes. Others' cheeks too were moist. I felt a barrage of mixed emotions – gratitude, nostalgia, regret, delight. We owed this kindness to a Mrs Kawamoto, we later discovered. She and her husband had run a Japanese bakery in Vancouver. But now he, a *gambariya*, was at Angler. In the unhappiness of those war years, this is one of the few pleasantly memorable scenes.

In retrospect, I am somewhat thankful for my experience of jail. There I was able to make contact with something previously unknown to me – the human being stripped of all that determines his positive self-image. I myself had a taste of the lowest point of human existence, the powerlessness and the shame. For a man to experience this is not an easy thing. But the lesson is an important one. I was able, for the first time, to empathize with people who live life at the rock bottom.

Thus for some three weeks we experienced the utter boredom of an uneventful existence. We wondered when our removal orders would come. Every day there was abundant conjecture

about our future confinement. Finally, on August 27 we
departed for Angler. It was after 7 pm when the Japanese
women and children who were still left in Vancouver gathered
at the CPR station to see us off. In a now sadly familiar scene,
colourful handkerchieves waved, some high, some low, against
the twilight backdrop. 'Be careful,' 'Gambare,' and sometimes
a brave 'Banzai,' were shouted enthusiastically. And from the
midst of this noisy crowd milling about, the train slowly pulled
away from the platform.

> Many passed this way,
> My countrymen.
> This train whistle
> They must have heard, and passed.
> Their feelings come to me.

Transcontinental removal

'WHAT SORT OF PLACE is this Angler to which we are going?' This question was no doubt uppermost in the mind of each of the fifty-odd others, as it was in mine. Angler was where German prisoners had formerly been kept and was located deep in the bush of northern Ontario. Such was the extent of our knowledge. Beyond this, however, I already had a negative impression of the atmosphere of an internment camp: I had heard about a recent shooting incident at Petawawa. There, after 7 pm, the inmates were not permitted to leave the buildings, and guards with machine guns watched from their towers. One night, fighting broke out. The accounts that finally filtered through to us were unclear as to the cause: perhaps, in the absence of any real news, the inmates had disagreed about the course of the war. At any rate the dissension must have been great, for the fighting burst out into the compound. The guards shone searchlights and shouted, asking what the commotion was about. Getting no reply, they fired what must have been only warning shots, since no one was hurt. Still, learning of this incident increased our natural anxiety.

Now, as the train slowly pulled out of Vancouver, I watched

the face of the city gradually changing in the dusk. Though we had not lived in Vancouver, my family and I had made many trips there from Woodfibre. Its skyscrapers were familiar landmarks, and many of its streets and shops had been the scene of happy family outings. I wondered when I would see it again, in a time of peace. For a long time I pressed my face against the windowpane.

The train now gathered speed. Within an hour I was gazing with brimming emotion at the farmlands of the Fraser valley, which had been opened up not so long before by Japanese pioneers. I had a personal attachment to the area because, when in my mid-teens I had first come from Japan, I had worked for over two years on my uncle's berry farm near Hammond ...

I had been born the second son of a rice farmer on the island of Kyushu, Japan. Since my elder brother had been in line to inherit the farm, my prospects had been poor. I had, however, this uncle who owned a farm in Canada, and he used to correspond with my father. One day my father asked me if I wanted to emigrate to Canada. My uncle was prepared to sponsor me. Though only fourteen at the time, I leapt at the chance.

Dots of light from the farmhouses and the highway shone through the foliage of the apple trees. My eyes tingled at the thrust of nostalgia. Thoroughly fatigued in mind and body, I succumbed to what felt like a short nap. When my eyes opened, the early dawn of summer was already showing palely in the eastern skies. Soon the bright morning sun was visible beyond the trees rushing past the windows. By midday the sun beat down mercilessly; we were then crossing over the Columbia River, whose waters sparkled in the bright light.

There in the Rockies the sharply cut rock face often closed in on the train from either side. The terrain was familiar from my days in the road camps to the north, but now I was seeing it from a different perspective as I passed through in a train. I spent that afternoon gazing upon the Rockies and wondering what lay beyond them to the east.

While we slept, the train left British Columbia behind. In the early hours of the twenty-ninth, in a dreamlike state, I was vaguely aware of passing through Calgary. Thereafter, as I became more awake, I had the impression of a valley opening up on either side into ever widening farmlands. The sky lightened and I saw the splendid vista that greets all travellers by rail who cross from west to east the expansive Canadian continent. As the vast prairies spread out before me, an indescribable excitement danced in my heart. Here and there I spotted farmhouses surrounded by trees. In the fields the tall golden grasses, their tips bent heavy with seed, quietly signalled the approach of autumn ...

Having decided to go to my uncle's farm in BC, I had enrolled at a school of agriculture, at the same time working hard to save money for the fare. During the next two years I often stood on the shore of the inland sea Suo Nada, dreaming of farmlands as vast as the ocean. Someday I would own such lands in faraway Canada, not a tiny farm like the farms of Japan.

At Medicine Hat I heard the loud whistle of a factory calling its men to work. I thought of my second home, Woodfibre. There, right up to the very day of evacuation, the factory whistle had called me to work each morning, and had released me each evening. For twenty years that sound had strangely given me hope and the resolution to work hard each day. I had worked contentedly in that isolated town since the age of nineteen. I recalled particularly the first eight years of that period, the springtime of my life, which I had spent without romantic love.

I noticed that the climate was different from that of the west coast. The prairies had a continental type of heat. From early morning the sun beat down fiercely on the grasslands. Yet beside the Medicine Hat station I spotted delicate wild flowers proudly blooming in late-summer glory. A soft breeze blew in through the train window and brought me their faint perfume, a momentary solace for my lonesome travel-weariness.

Now no matter how far we travelled there was nothing on the horizon to block our view. The endless prairies had opened up before us. Large cumulus clouds floated above the distant horizon, a daringly pure mass of white on the expanse of blue. I was astonished at the vastness of the land – a thousand miles could be taken in at a glance!

That made me think of tiny Japan. I thought of how Canada was underpopulated whereas Japan was overpopulated. Such a difference seemed so unfair. Granted, there was not much that could be done about chance inequities. But if countries with surplus land kept out the people of countries with too little land, was it not a crime? Should such fortunate countries not permit more immigration? For our part, we Japanese could do something about our population problem. Despite evacuation, despite internment, I was still convinced that more of us should emigrate overseas, begin to see ourselves as citizens of the world, and gain the trust of other peoples. This would be a constructive measure.

Gazing at the Canadian prairies that appeared to go on to the ends of the earth, I wondered where a war could possibly be in progress. Yet because I was distracted by anxiety, even those thousand miles, though they took the whole of that day and half that night to traverse, rushed by as in a dream; only two stops, at Moose Jaw and Regina, were long enough not to escape notice. Eventually, however, as if returning from another realm, the train pulled into Winnipeg.

> Wet with rain,
> Night train window.
> Reflected
> Prairie city
> Lights.

The morning of August 30 found us in Ontario. The sky was clear, but this had no cheering effect on my spirits that day. In a few hours we heard that the next stop would be Angler. Now I wondered in earnest what sort of place it would be. I peered out apprehensively from the window of the speeding train. Before long I felt the train slowing down, until the shrill blow of the whistle announced our arrival.

First weeks at Angler

THE DAZZLING MIDDAY SUN beat strongly upon our backs as we got off the train at the little station at Angler. The heat and the dryness of the atmosphere were dizzying. Through squinting eyes I saw the clear blue of the sky stretching all the way out to a distant horizon. The only object in view was what I took to be an army barracks, surrounded by acre upon acre of outcrops and hilly forested land.

About one hundred soldiers were there waiting to escort our small party to the internment camp. We were greeted by rifles with bayonets, some now pointed at us. Picking up our belongings, we proceeded to drag along on train-numbed legs for some twenty minutes. This brought us before imposing wooden gates, about sixteen feet high and covered with barbed wire. They opened with an ominous creak. One step within, and our lives would be completely in the hands of others.

I entered with great uneasiness. I found myself within a large compound enclosed by a double fence. The fences were some ten feet apart, as high as the gates, and topped with barbed wire. Crossing the compound with our guards, we were greeted by some fifty internees; that was heartening, although, as they were *gambariya*, I did not feel at one with them. What surprised me was that each man's shirt bore a bright red circle on the back. And each inmate seemed to sport it proudly as the rising sun of the Japanese flag.

> Covering the entire back,
> The rising sun on their shirts
> The inmates are made to wear.
> Ecstatic are the wearers –
> But what a fine target.

We were soon ushered into a building that was one large empty hall. There each man was required to strip to his underwear to show that he concealed nothing on his person. All cash and valuables were taken from us. Next we were issued regulation dress. There were two sets of blue denim day wear, the shirt having the red circle on the back, and the pants having a red stripe down the outside of each leg; a blue cap with a red crown completed the outfit. Then there were two sets of night wear, off-white pyjamas. Finally we were given a pillow and a blanket. By the time all this was accomplished, evening was fast approaching.

After supper I found I was very sleepy. It was largely from nervous strain, but as well I was physically fatigued from the train trip of over two thousand miles. I did not have the energy to remain standing and dropped exhausted on my bed. Acquaintances from among those earlier interned came in turn to greet me. We exchanged warm handshakes and rejoiced together that we were still safe.

At around nine I stretched out, but sleep would not come. It seemed that even with my eyes closed I could see the piercing white light of the lamp outside the window, one of a number of such glaring lamps placed at about one-hundred-foot intervals along the fence. At some point, however, I must have dropped off to sleep, for soon I was having a terrible nightmare. The most threatening feature of the dream was its locale, the Immigration Building jail, subjected to gruesome distortions. Suddenly my eyes popped open. Standing in the gloom beside my bed was a soldier on night guard, staring at me. I thought I must have let out a wail, for I could see a wry expression on his face. He withdrew as quickly as he had appeared.

For two or three days after arriving at Angler I had the illusion of still riding in the train. I had difficulty orienting myself in the present because of the succession of changes and emotional upheavals of my recent past. Leaving Descoigne in eager anticipation of reunion with my loved ones, being shocked at Hope by the probability that I would not be sent to Greenwood, the fruitless negotiations at Slocan, the privation of the Immigration Building jail, and the dreamlike transcontinental removal – the miles upon miles of one move after another, culminating in the arrival at Angler – scenes crowded together and revolved in my mind, as if in a magic lantern show, until dizziness overcame me. Yet beneath all this, at some centre of consciousness, I knew that I was now an interned person. And this realization so threatened my mind that I escaped into long hours of sleep. Only intermittently did I awake, always to the painful reality of my new situation, which I fought to expel from my thoughts.

The balm of sleep did its work. In the next few days I felt a gradual return to something like my normal self. And as was usually the way with me, I was first brought out of my depression by curiosity about my new surroundings. Soon whatever came to my eyes and ears fed the eager activity of my imagination.

The camp was located deep in bush country and seemed, besides, to lie in a large natural depression in the land. The least obstructed view was to the southeast, where on a clear morning I could watch the sun gradually illuminate the field.

The internment camp at Angler, north of Lake Superior:
morning roll call, winter 1942

Generally, though, because of rises in the land on all sides, I
could not see to any distance. It seemed, however, that at
Angler there were only the army barracks and the internment
camp. There seemed to be no town or even scattered houses in
the vicinity. Only because of the army post did the transcontinental train stop from time to time. I thought that the transcontinental highway must run somewhere parallel to the
railway, but I had no idea where it could be. The tidy rows of
the barracks were about five hundred feet to the west of our
compound. And beyond them lay the railway, at that point
running north to south. Although the camp was a twenty-
minute walk from the station, I could sometimes hear the
whistle or see the dancing rise of black smoke. Thinking that
that train had brought me all the way from Vancouver, I clung
to these meagre links to my past.

Further beyond, to the west-southwest, was a lake, the great Lake Superior, as I was told. In that season it was blocked from view by the full foliage of the trees. Yet I knew it was there. All day long, flocks of seagulls flew about overhead. I welcomed them as the only visitors from the outside world. To the east and to the south, dense coniferous forests blocked the view. To the north, grassy fields ran out to some low hills beyond which nothing was visible. I was impressed that they had found such a desolate locale, so suitable for an internment camp. It was difficult to get one's bearings with any degree of accuracy. In fact, it was difficult to determine at what point this unreal world within the enclosure made contact with the outside world of everyday reality.

I soon turned my attention upon the features of the five acres that lay within the large five-sided enclosure. The only entrance was just to the southwest of the northernmost point of the compound. Ranged along the full length of three of the sides of the enclosure were wood-frame buildings with plaster-board walls. The six public buildings were of various sizes. The three along one of the longer sides of the enclosure, that having the gates, were to the right of those gates as one entered: first, the small detention shed; next, another small building, partitioned so as to house the camp leader's office and another office, which was later to be the canteen; and finally, at some distance, the large building where we had been examined upon arrival, and which later served as the recreation hall. The other three buildings were along one of the shorter sides of the enclosure, to the left of the gates as one entered: the large infirmary; beyond it, the larger kitchen and mess hall, occupying the northeast corner of the compound; and, tucked away behind the latter, a small building, partitioned so as to house the barbershop and what was later to be the library. To the right of this, working southwest along the longest side of the enclosure, that opposite the gates, were ten large dormitory

One of the H-shaped huts that housed eighty men

buildings, rectangular in shape and arranged in a row, side by side in tenement style.

These dormitory buildings stood oriented northwest-southeast. They were parallel lengthwise, in pairs joined by a passageway in the middle to form a capital H. Each building, or more accurately wing, had three doors to the outside, one at each end and one in the middle opposite the passageway to the other wing. Inside a wing were forty bunk beds placed along the windows, two coal-burning potbellied stoves, one toward either end, and, near them, tables and benches. The passageway housed toilets, showers, and the large tubs of a laundry area.

Internment life involved some work, about a half-day's worth, when it was available. A typical assignment was fetching provisions or coal from the station. Work crews also went outside the camp to cut wood for the kitchen stoves. I took part in such errands only a few times before they were completely taken over by the younger men. Some men were permanently assigned to cooking duties, others to duties in the mess hall or in the infirmary. Still others did maintenance in carpentry or in plumbing. Of course we took turns keeping our dormitory buildings clean. Thus all the work of the camp was done by us internees.

With the work thus rationed, there was any amount of free time. Newspapers, radio, movies, were not available; even letter-writing was severely restricted. The hours were whiled away in walking around the compound, reading books, talking in small groups, and playing cards. Later on, judo, kendo, and other sports were organized and many took part enthusiastically in the daily practices. By then, too, the better educated internees were holding classes for the younger ones in history, literature, calligraphy, and other subjects. All in the camp came to have great respect for these instructors, who gave freely of their time and talents. But the fact remained that we were not free to do what we wanted to do. This was to prove especially hard on the youths, who therefore gradually assumed more of the work in order to keep busy.

As an attempt at political organization, a group was set up to represent us. Made up of nearly three dozen from our ranks, this committee acted as go-between for all eight hundred of us internees and the authorities. It was headed by a camp leader elected from its number. Other members included the elected heads of the dormitory wings; those in charge of the kitchen, the infirmary, and the other public facilities; those who assigned the various work details; the various instructors; and the news reporter.

As best it could, then, the camp tried to organize itself as a little community. Despite this, there inside the barbed wire fence, completely isolated from the real world outside, I was not alone in feeling ill at ease. During the evacuation process, I had had my attention fixed by the successive events. But once physically settled in one place where I would probably be kept for some time, I experienced the revival of anxieties that were by then only too familiar. Yet at the same time I was conscious of a strong will to live life fully. Mere existence would not do. I resolved to think and to act positively, to prepare for a happier future with my family.

Adaptation difficulties

AWAKENED AT DAWN by the summons of a bugle, I would make my bed and go to breakfast, in the first of two shifts. At the mess hall I would join the line and wait my turn for the handout. The fare was always the same, always simple – a small glass of juice, two slices of toast, a little butter and jam, a cup of tea. It always left me feeling hungry.

When I went outdoors after breakfast, a new world seemed to open up before my eyes. Angler's morning display in vibrant colours was truly splendid. The sun that glowed beyond the fields filled me with ecstasy. As at the road camps in the Rockies I had taken solace from the beauty of nature, so now in this new setting I turned from sadness to absorb greedily all that nature afforded my senses. I felt cleansed as deep draughts of fresh air filled first nostrils and then lungs, until a pleasing satiety came over me. In such a mood I could momentarily achieve a calm acceptance of my lot. I would quietly proceed to the site of the eight o'clock roll call.

For exercise I made it a practice most days to walk around the perimeter of the compound, along the oval track that had been worn by many others. I walked at three different times,

after breakfast, in the afternoon, and in the evening, a total of
at least three miles. During a walk my stomach would habitually complain of hunger. I learned to drink a glass of water to
quiet its demands. I knew hunger well in those days, though of
course not to the point where my health was endangered. Perhaps my stomach's uneasiness had as much to do with the
unrelenting anxiety I had experienced since the moment when
my family had been rent apart. How often in a day did my
thoughts revert to Greenwood, which I had known only for a
few minutes at a railroad station. I could envision Yukie and
Toshimi living there in as much loneliness as I was feeling at
Angler. 'If anything were to happen to either of them, how
soon would I be notified? And aren't my circumstances such
that I wouldn't be allowed to go to them?' When my thoughts
took such a turn, I fought hard to pull them back in a positive
direction.

One morning at around ten, two weeks after our arrival, the
familiar figures of our camp leader Tanaka and, behind him,
the camp commander appeared on the scene. In the early days
we had a camp inspection twice a week, although as time went
on it took place less frequently. We usually stood around outside during the inspection of our quarters. The commander's
expression as he passed was habitually stern. But that morning
I happened to be indoors after my walk, and I noted that he
seemed to be in a different mood. He picked up a *kokeshi
ningyo* (a Japanese ornamental wooden doll) from someone's
pillow, and his face momentarily relaxed into a smile.

Having received no mail since my arrival, I had been looking
daily for the delivery that would bring a reply to the letter I
had written Yukie. We internees were allowed to write only
one letter a month. We were issued a single standard sheet,
about the size of today's airletter. Only the centre third, about
six or seven lines' worth, was marked out for the message.
Moreover this section was lined like graph paper, each square

to accommodate one Japanese character; thus the number of syllables, and therefore words, was limited. One necessarily experimented with rough drafts. Yet I found that unless I made the message very short, I came to the end of the space with only a fraction of what I intended to say written. And then I had no idea how much of that the camp censors would delete. Still, I had sent off my first letter to Yukie.

Our letters had crossed, for on this same mid-September morning I received the first letter from my wife in three months, since one sent to Descoigne road camp. I hastily tore open the envelope. What a disappointment! So many words had been excised that the letter was totally incomprehensible. I had heard that only news of the war or projections of the course of it would be censored. My anger mounted. I thought that, although we were the 'enemy,' the authorities need not have condoned such cruel excess of the censoring guidelines. The position of censor had to be held by someone with an extensive knowledge of Japanese. I got what small comfort I could by wryly commenting to myself, 'A true Japanese could not have perpetrated such an insensitive hacking job!'

At a time when I was experiencing great difficulty in adjusting, the six others who had families in Greenwood seemed to be adapting well to the situation. (The eight with families in Kaslo had been released after only two weeks' internment, following the intercession of the United Church of that town. But the Catholic Church of Greenwood had decided against a similar move.) I felt envious of my carefree fellow inmates. For me, day followed upon day of discontent. But I kept reassuring myself that in any case I would not remain where I was for very long. Soon I would be moved to confinement elsewhere, or be sent back to a victorious Japan. In those days notions could still be entertained of an eventual victory for Japan, since the limited news we heard was favourable to Japan. In reflections of later years I have become convinced that this news was carefully slanted in order to encourage the *gambariya*. The camp reporter was given a copy of an English-language newspaper and could select what he wanted from it to post in translation. At any rate, at that time I awaited the day of any change.

I did not have any immediate insight into the atmosphere of the camp. But as the days passed, I gradually came to know the general mood of the majority of the eight hundred. It was definitely not easy. Like the men at the road camps, most of these men were taciturn and held themselves back. Yet there was a substantial number who talked big in a bid for others' regard; this bravado was a marked characteristic of the outspoken *gambariya*. Such men believed absolutely in Japan's eventual victory and expected personal postwar compensation from a defeated Canada. There was an important difference between men such as these, who had sought confinement to protest the outrage of the evacuation, and those of us who had been brought to Angler much against our will. And that difference overruled the fact that the *gambariya* and the men in my position did hold some views in common.

My state of mind in those early days is best shown by an excerpt from the diary entry for the day that I am setting before you:

Completely at a loss I walk listlessly, following the fence around and around. It troubles me that anxiety is now always written on my face. The brilliant sunlight streaming down upon me does not expel my dejection. I am only very lonely.

This afternoon a pair of screeching seagulls flew into the compound, circling lower and lower over my head, almost brushing against it time and time again. I wondered if they knew of my captivity and flaunted their freedom to tease me. Soon they disappeared, and in the clear autumn sky only the occasional wisp of white cloud floated past.

How much longer I must stay here cannot be known. How much longer must I stay, with my skinny body getting ever leaner? How much longer, wearing the rising sun on my back, advocating patriotism to my fatherland with my fellow prisoners, the *gambariya*, who are holding out determinedly here in camp?

Even though at this moment I feel bereft of any love in this world, I want to keep a warmth within my heart for the day of reunion with Yukie and Toshimi.

I had entered a period of my life in which, whenever my anxiety became acute, I opened my Bible. I had ordered it from Japan when I was twenty, at the urging of a zealous young Christian. But with that youth's return to Japan soon thereafter, and with neither church nor minister in the Japanese community of Woodfibre, my Bible study had fallen by the wayside. Yet so many years later, when my removal to the road camp was imminent, I had carefully placed the Bible in the bottom of my bag.

When I had first taken up the Bible again at Angler, I had not been much impressed. Still, as I had continued to read to beguile the daily tedium, some impression had been left little by little. Meanwhile I was daily facing the unalterable fact of my unjust imprisonment. And beneath this immediate concern lay a more fundamental problem: the true nature of the human condition eluded my understanding. Or rather, that view of it that had stood me in good stead for most of my adult life now no longer sufficed. I was confused. It was imperative that I find some answers soon. The Bible beckoned with the offer of new hope and courage.

They that wait upon the Lord shall renew their strength; they shall mount up with wings as eagles; they shall run, and not be weary; and they shall walk, and not faint.

It was pure chance that these words of Isaiah 40:31 caught my eye. They had an immeasurable effect upon me spiritually. My heart was deeply moved. Had those been normal times, I might have passed over the words with little interest. But now I read them over repeatedly, and pondered upon them. Contact with them seemed to mark a dividing line between my previous life and the life that now opened out before me. My soul made a shift in a positive direction, in search of truth.

I had never read the Bible with such eagerness as I then began to do. Genesis, Exodus, Leviticus, I followed the books of the Old Testament in order. For one as inexperienced as I, this was work requiring a great deal of patience. Yet I was rewarded by a sense of touching upon a new world, an effect doubtless compounded by the fact of my being an Easterner.

Bible reading, then, formed a large part of my daily routine. When I took a break from studies, I stretched out on the grass and watched the drifting of clouds, feeling therein the flow of my heart. Hours passed unnoticed as I lay in aimless reflection.

A couple of weeks had passed since my arrival, yet I had no real knowledge of the topography of the environs. What little news we had from the outside world was of the war. There was no one to tell us anything about the area that we inhabited. I knew only what I gathered from viewing the scenery in all directions. The morning sun climbing in the northeastern sky and the evening sun sinking in the northwest gave me some bearings. But that was all.

The haiku club

THE BUSH surrounding the camp was sleeping peacefully in the early-October morning. A lone crow had winged towards the east, cawing as it went. A flock of gulls had approached from beyond the trees to the south and had passed noisily overhead. Now no sound violated the quiet dignity of the morning.

Suddenly sharp commands broke the silence. The voice was that of one Kawaguchi. Under his guidance, some hundred and fifty eager young men began the thirty-minute calisthenics session that took place on most fair days. Many of us gathered round to watch. I liked to watch the intent faces of the other onlookers fill with pleasure. The exercises completed, the noise was abruptly cut off, and quiet was restored to the camp.

I turned towards the bush beyond the fence. Its ochre had been deepening day by day. The leaves, sprinkled with morning dew, sparkled like a rich brocade. I was conscious of a sadness in the honking of the high flying geese. The wind, which whistled through the fence, was quite chilly. I knew that many emotion-laden tanka would be born of these signs of the deepening of autumn.

That afternoon I went to the haiku club meeting. Within the first month of our stay at Angler, one of our group by the name of Baisetsu had started the club. Because of the tedium of the camp life, it had quickly attracted members. The circumstance of confinement made for the production of many highly subjective haiku.

The procedure of the club activity was as follows. During the week each member submitted his haiku. All the haiku were written on one sheet by a member assigned to the task. Baisetsu then corrected these haiku, which were for him anonymous, and picked out the best.

Now, at the start of the meeting, Baisetsu repeated the haiku topic that had been announced at the last meeting, 'the birthday of the Meiji Emperor.' He then went through each submitted haiku line by line, giving a detailed explanation, making critical comments, and suggesting changes. Meanwhile the fifteen members present waited excitedly, each wondering if his haiku had been selected as the best. Or failing that, perhaps it had made the top three, or at least the top ten for honourable mention. After going over all the haiku, Baisetsu read out in order of merit the ones he had chosen. After each was read, the transcriber revealed the name of the poet. The topic for the next meeting, 'the milky way,' was announced. With that the meeting was brought to a close.

I was in good spirits because my haiku had been in the top ten. This was to happen often; sometimes I even made the top three. I enjoyed composing haiku and learned much from the practice, although my preference was for the tanka form.

> Wild chrysanthemums' perfume,
> Clear blue sky,
> Meiji Day!

The haiku club was a great success and attracted more members as it continued. It survived through the closing of Angler and the removal of the remaining *gambariya* to a smaller camp at Moose Jaw, and right up to the closing of that camp at the end of the war. The best haiku written during its existence were collected in an anthology called *Tessaku no Seki*, 'loneliness within the barbed wire fence.' This volume comprises some two hundred pages of haiku all individually handwritten by the contributors. Some three dozen copies were made – a considerable job. And especially considering where it was put together, the product is a highly respectable piece of work. The efforts of the haiku comrades, spanning nearly four years, have thus left a brilliant remembrance of life at Angler internment camp. We who are fortunate enough to possess a copy hold one page of Japanese Canadian wartime history.

Aside from those days when the haiku club met, many indistinguishable days now followed. It was not until an afternoon in late October that it fell to my lot to take part in what was for me a novel experience. The assignment was to cut wood for the kitchen stoves. Five guards led ten of us out through the camp gates. It was the first time I had been allowed out of the compound since my arrival at the end of August. Walking in a troop of men bearing axes and saws, I was reminded of happier days in the road camps at Yellowhead and Descoigne. There too we had not been free to leave; but I had since realized how much I had undervalued the semblance of freedom afforded by the absence of a fence. Now, here outside the compound, it seemed that everyone's spirits were uplifted and his footfalls lighter.

A twenty-minute walk brought us to a black spruce grove to the northeast. We set to work eagerly. The huge trees yielded to our blows reluctantly, falling thunderously at last.

> Primeval forest!
> Feeling as though in violation,
> Cutting down standing trees
> Before watchful guards.
> Cutting firewood.

Since the late-October air was cold, we chopped off the smallest branches for fuel, gathered dry dead wood from the forest floor, and started a fire. Soon it gave off a comforting warmth. We gathered round and talked excitedly. How Yellowhead days revived in my memory!

Likely surprised by a sudden blaze of the fire, a flock of wild geese passing overhead broke formation. I was reminded of a history lesson from my schoolboy days. There had once been a famous Japanese army commander whose renown was partly due to his humility in continuing to consult the strategists. This humility was rewarded when, one day, he recalled having heard that the sudden flight of birds could reveal the location of a hidden enemy; he thus was able to save the day. I reflected that even an enemy would not venture to the desolate environs of Angler.

As the fire burned ever more vigorously, the leaping flames were reflected in the numerous pools of clear water of the swampy area we were in. Drawn at first by the reflections, I peered intently into the water. Not the shadow of a fish was visible. 'If these were the swamps of Japan, minnows would abound,' I thought lonesomely.

Wishing to take the fullest advantage of being outside the compound, I took stock of my surroundings. There was no sign of a building or of a road. 'Even if someone dared a night escape, he would stand little chance of success in the darkness of bush and swamp,' I thought ruefully. Yet even such a dismal thought could not spoil the pleasant half-day the woodcutting assignment had unexpectedly afforded.

Seagulls often flew over the compound and always were a brief diversion from my solitude. It seemed strange that while seagulls were a common sight, I could see no lake in any direction. Meanwhile, the colourful birches, poplars, maples, and other autumn trees that brightened the surrounding bush daily dropped more leaves. Grey silhouettes soon laced the horizon.

At last there came the day when through them I could make out a glistening blue surface. The sight was all the more uplifting for having been so long withheld. I was delighted that the natural process of the falling of the leaves had discovered to me this distant view. Now each day in my three routine walks, when I came to the spot whence the deep blue was most visible, I paused to stare at length. My thoughts returned to Suo Nada, the inland sea near my birthplace in Fukuoka. The lake now in view and the old association combined to stir in me a desire to write tanka in tribute to the sublimity of bodies of water.

> Voice of the waves
> Calling.
> A quickening in my breast.
> Unwittingly uttered,
> 'Suo Nada.'

The succession of uneventful days stretched on, and before long we were well into November. Particularly in the morning and evening the cold north wind whistled through the camp. In those days I continued to pace the oval track along the fence. I found myself thinking back nostalgically even to such recent times as the warmer days of September, when butterflies had sported about the wire mesh of the fence, and dandelions had bloomed in profusion at its base.

At this time a quantity of books arrived from the Japanese library of prewar Vancouver. We who had been short of news and reading material welcomed the chance for mental and emotional enrichment. From the books, which covered a wide range of subjects, I selected many I liked, all books of tanka and of prose classics – *Manyōshū, Kokinshū, Genji Monogatari, Takuboku Zenshū*, and others. As it grew colder I spent more of the day indoors, reading by the dormitory stove.

Now and then, as my concentration lapsed, I became aware of the voices of the old men who chatted animatedly whilst warming themselves. A phrase or two of their talk sometimes would set me off on a new train of thought. Often the *gambariya's* enthusiasm for their cause made me feel my own lack of a cause even more. I was plagued by perplexing questions and deep doubts. In the recent past I had been dropped to the depths of despair, where for a time I had languished. Having recovered enough to begin searching, I had sought ultimate answers. I had become convinced that these lay in the Bible. I had resolved that I would read it all the way through to the end. At first, spurred on by the spirit of investigation, I had tackled the project energetically. But as I had encountered more and more that I could not understand, my interest had flagged. I had come to think that it was indeed too difficult to comprehend Christianity just by reading the Bible by oneself. Yet still I persevered in reading a little of the Scriptures each day.

Meanwhile, the course of the war seemed to have been changing, both in the Pacific and in Europe, in a direction that I had never really faced as a possibility. Even to my limited perception – as the news came to us through the reporter – it looked bad for Japan. I craved access to more news.

In those unsettled times it was not unusual for my eyes to open suddenly in the dead of night. Then they would invariably be drawn towards the light of the bright lamp at the fence. Its unnatural glare could still arouse an eerie sensation in me. The bush country all around us lay in darkness. On one such occasion, I lay awake reflecting that there were few who knew that such a place as the camp existed. I felt that we had been forsaken by the rest of the world. A heaven full of stars twinkled above; the milky way glittered like an obi of Nishijin weave (a famous weave produced in Kyoto), spanning the firmament. Heaven and earth were hushed with a silence as of death. I felt keenly the vastness of the universe, no less of the earth itself, against which the insignificance of my existence was brought home to me. But my individual unimportance aside, I wondered what was becoming of the human race.

Winter shut-ins

DAYS AND WEEKS passed by slowly, but before we knew it autumn had given way to winter. So far December had been cold every day. There was already some excitement in the air as Christmas, our first at Angler, approached. At Woodfibre, Christmas had usually been without snow. Angler had already had snow in November, and now the land was white as far as the eye could see.

Toshimi had never yet experienced a fatherless Christmas. How neglected she would surely feel. My immediate desire was to send her a toy, but I quickly realized that this was impossible from within the camp. I then wanted to write her a long letter explaining why her father could not send her a present. But even with letters we were not at complete liberty. I spent the better part of a day brooding upon the frustrations of my situation. That night, toward midnight, fierce winter blasts hit the roofs and sides of our dormitory buildings. Once wakened by the sound, I could not stop thinking of Yukie and Toshimi.

Soon it was Christmas Eve, 1942. From the barracks came the loud voices of a chorus of lively singers – the soldiers, heedless of the war being fought on other shores. The uproar mounted and persisted. The quiet of our dormitory was in telling contrast. Though we were of the one human race, and only the double fence separated us from them, we internees led a very different life. I felt acutely the unfairness of the contrast between the free and the constrained. We could not even set foot outside the dormitory after 7 pm. If one did, there would be a warning question from a watchtower; if that were unheeded, there would be no help for it if the offender were shot. I was constantly uneasy, aware, if only barely consciously, of those ready rifles of the guards.

Within the compound, Christmas Day differed little from any other. At dinner, however, there appeared small fancy cakes and cookies. Wondering how they had come to grace our table, we quickly took our seats. Mr Nobuoka, the steward, explained before we ate. These dainty pastries, enough for all eight hundred, were from our countrymen in Greenwood and Kaslo. Thousands of miles separated us from our benefactors, but I had a sense of our still being as one, as brothers and sisters.

That evening, the singing from the barracks was even louder than it had been the night before. This time, however, a gathering, though a more modest one, also took place within our dormitory. It was common for four or five youths to gather at a bed to chat, laugh, and sing. That evening, at around eight, such a group gathered at a bed near mine. Perhaps the young men were reminiscing about happier Christmases at home in the Vancouver of an earlier day. Or perhaps they were thinking of their girlfriends far away. The sing-song started. 'Furusato,' 'Haha Koishi,' 'Shanhai Musume,' 'Sendo Kōuta' – one after the other they sang the popular Japanese tunes. A youth of eighteen had the bed next to mine. He sat listening with a faraway look in his eyes. I could not know what memories the songs brought back for him, but soon he was struggling to fight back tears. In the dim light of the dormitory, I looked around at the faces of the hapless young men and felt pity.

After lights out at ten, some youths were still whispering amongst themselves. In the soldiers' barracks, which had been so noisy until then, the singing and laughing gradually subsided as it grew late, until finally all festivity ceased. It was then a completely silent night. In the dormitory just one tiny light cast its feeble rays into the large room. Before long the night guard, smelling strongly of whisky, entered for an early bed check. He was someone I readily recognized: tall, stout, red-faced, he was an imposing figure under any circumstances; pompous and habitually rough in his dealings with us, he was especially unpopular. Lying very still, I watched him. Grinning broadly, he distractedly made the rounds and departed.

I welcomed 1943 with a silent prayer to the first sunrise of the year. And I prayed for the safety of my beloved fatherland and of my parents and other kin, from whom I had had no communication since Pearl Harbor. Opening the window, I breathed deeply of the cold air and viewed the endless expanse of pastel sky. I felt a constriction in my throat as I reflected upon how my physical state and circumstances had altered in less than a year. I thought the camp a truly bleak place.

Yet the camp was enabling me to experience a life of simplicity – plain meals, few clothes, next to no amusements – and to know it as not a bad thing. In ordinary life, had I not carried about an excess of unnecessary things? By contrast, the camp lifestyle was refreshingly simple. One day I would be released into a life of freedom. Then I would be active to my heart's content. And the narrow existence of the camp – depending upon my attitude, could it not serve as an excellent preparation for those later years? It was, then, truly New Year's Morn. I felt my heart racing out to embrace the most optimistic view of things possible. Thus, in good spirits, I left

Walking the circuit of the double fence for exercise

the dormitory for the mess hall. The cold was the most severe
that we had yet experienced at Angler. It felt as though
needles pierced my ears and the tip of my nose. Thanks to the
cautioning words of a fellow internee, I escaped frostbite. It
was, he told me, forty degrees below zero.

Now week after week the harsh winter of northern Ontario
kept the camp even more closed in from the outside world. To
escape from being cooped up indoors, I took advantage of any
relatively warmer days to resume my walks around the compound. On one such day in February, I awoke to the sight of
huge snowflakes drifting gracefully to the ground in the calm
air. After breakfast, I went for a walk in that white world.
Several inches of new snow had already accumulated on the path.
As I walked along at a brisk pace, I heard from somewhere the
faintly audible chanting of 'wassho-wassho, wassho-wassho,'
accompanying muffled footfalls. I turned fully around but saw
no one. The rhythmic sound, however, came nearer and

nearer. Before long there emerged from behind the dormitory buildings and headed towards me seven youths repeating the 'wassho-wassho,' with its strangely hypnotic quality. The large flakes now fell more thickly. As the runners passed me I saw flakes land on their flushed faces and momentarily keep their intricate forms before melting away. In my mind the youths seemed to be of the famous company of *The Forty-seven Ronin*. They were of the pure of heart, like those loyal samurai who had vindicated the honour of their lord in the full knowledge that they would pay for the deed with their lives. The faces of these youthful *gambariya* seemed to assert an equal determination, though in a different cause. I could not help but admire that determination, even though the cause was not mine.

Throughout the winter, the benches placed by the dormitory stoves were the centres of indoor activity. I, who waking and sleeping had books on my mind, tried reading a variety of matter. But *Manyōshū* and *Kokinshū* absorbed me most. And I never tired of the fine tanka of *Takuboku Zenshū*, although I had read it through many times. Takuboku, a prodigy, was a famous poet though he had died young, in his late twenties. I had first been delighted by his tanka while still a schoolboy. They still gave me the best feeling of any tanka I knew.

The stoveside was, naturally enough, the scene of discussions full of conjectures about the war. What war news was reported to us by the designated committee member was of successive victories by the Japanese armed forces. Thus many *gambariya* were encouraged to say such things as, 'The Japanese have done it again! What did you expect?' They had made up their minds to Japan's eventual victory. They looked forward to the war's termination, when they expected to receive personal compensation and planned to go with it to a life of comfort in their fatherland.

One day in March a strange incident took place, which I recorded in my diary. Later I learned that similar scenes had begun to occur in the camp at about that time. As usual, I was reading at the stoveside. The conversation of some nearby men drifted in and out of my consciousness as my level of concentration fluctuated. The others of the group suddenly fell silent, leaving the voice of one, a middle-aged fellow, starkly audible. I was surprised to hear him voice the very suspicions that had lately begun to spring up in my mind. I heard him say, 'I don't trust the war news we get.' He continued, 'I've been thinking I'd like to get a job and leave here soon.'

No sooner had the last word left his lips than K., an old man, said: 'What's this? What the hell are you saying? You're a damn traitor!' Then he quickly changed tack to add, 'If you're so keen on leaving, get the hell out now!' He then addressed H., another old man, who sat across from him, saying, 'Am I not right, H.?'

H., being careful to lock eyes with K., replied, 'I'm with you, friend.' He said this nodding his head and patting K.'s shoulder in further show of concurrence. Turning towards the middle-aged chap, who now hung his head, he shouted, 'Idiot!'

Drawn by the raised voices, others in the dormitory now approached the stoveside. The middle-aged man continued to be silent and visibly shrank beneath the stares of the company. Suddenly he bolted from their midst. Soon three others of the original group left the strained atmosphere, quietly slipping away one by one. Those who had gathered round quickly dispersed, their expressions seeming to say that this, likely just another of the disputes common among the restive internees, held little interest. Only the old men K. and H. remained, strong in their mutual support. As they became engrossed in conversation, I slipped out for my afternoon walk, only too glad to escape into the cold fresh air.

A civilian casualty

EVEN TO THE CAMP, which had been shut in during an interminable winter, with the coming of April spring began slowly to make itself known. Now some days when I went outdoors I felt the warm sunshine spread relaxation throughout my body. How regenerative the springtime warmth was, despite where it was enjoyed. At night, too, there was a new stir in the air. Once I witnessed the pulsating luminosity of the aurora borealis spread across the pitch black sky. I longed to share the sight with my family.

April gave way to May. One morning, as I looked to the southeast, I saw a mist suspended above the field. I was reminded of a tanka by Kakinomoto no Hitomaro, found in the first volume of *Manyōshū*:

> To the east,
> In the fields, from the warm damp earth
> Steam rises.
> And when I glance around behind me
> I see the moon declining.

Now the mist of the field at Angler included me in its cool embrace. As I walked and walked in it, my eyelashes becoming damp, I experienced the not unpleasant sensation of fading away. The wind that soon bore the mist from the camp was a warm spring wind. 'Ah, yes, it is spring now,' I thought. 'Even to this cold north country, spring has unmistakably come.' I turned my head and saw the pale moon sinking in the western sky.

One day in early June, Isshu, a youth of some twenty years and a haiku club member, had an attack of appendicitis. The army doctor was to operate on him. As he was being carried off towards the barracks, Isshu cheerfully insisted that he would recover and be back with us in no time at all. But we heard the next morning that he had done badly after the operation and had died. I was shocked and inconsolable. I kept hearing his brave parting words.

The next afternoon, at our haiku club meeting, one seat, the one he usually occupied, remained vacant. The meeting over, I, now alone, walked along the fence, as I had often done in lively conversation with him. The enthusiasm he had shown came back to me. A novice with a passion for writing haiku, he had told me how he thought of them even in sleep. We had had many discussions about the composition of good haiku. I had often talked to him about Bashō. Isshu and I had come to share the theory that the poet must put into the haiku an impression of the object itself, in such a way that it comes as a shock to the reader's spirit. There beside the path were the bright yellow dandelions. I recalled how last autumn we had marvelled at the stunted dandelions encroaching upon the path, undaunted by the tread of many feet. I thought of how Isshu would return to my thoughts in the years to come. In recent months I had heard many accounts of tragedies of the war. They had been too great to be deeply felt. But the death of one who had been close to me in a common interest cut keenly.

That night I lay awake thinking of Isshu, then was carried into the more usual train of my night-time thought. On rainy nights, on quiet snowy nights, on windy nights when the building groaned – how often through the autumn and winter had I lain awake, lost in thought, clutching at memories of happier days with my family. That night, as these came to seem less and less real, I felt increasingly empty. All the love Yukie and Toshimi and I shared could not save me now. I became conscious of the darkness as endlessly spacious: in it my tiny self was engulfed. Then a crushing pressure seemed to close in from all about me. For a terrible moment I knew that this thing called self was completely alone in the infinite universe.

I had been brought to know that it was not for a human truly to rely upon another. For man cut a pitifully small figure indeed. How often through the ages must he have cried out at his impotence! Where, then, was the solution to one's need to reach out to something beyond oneself? I yearned to know. Christianity seemed to offer a solution. Yet for me to become a Christian demanded the repudiation of the many Japanese notions with which I had grown up. I still retained many ideas from the Japanese tradition, and specifically the Buddhist tenets. Conversion would be a large question indeed. It would, in any case, require considerable time. As it turned out, I was not to become a Christian until long after the experience at Angler.

Realization that in the camp even good medical care, something generally taken for granted, was not readily available, had brought life's daily uncertainty home to me. Again I resolved to do something, anything, about the circumstance of my internment.

That I had done nothing before this was quite explicable. I was still under constraint, of course. Beyond that, however, unable to overcome the effects of the environment and of the passage of time, I had, despite myself, succumbed to camp existence. From time to time, in self-reflection, I had marked my altered state and asked myself if it were all right.

Day followed upon day of tense inaction. And still I looked to my surroundings to provide the stimulation I so needed. Once during the change of season to summer, as I looked around me, my gaze lingered upon the rise to the northwest; Mount Kagu, in the vicinity of Nara, floated before me as if in a vision. Against the actual rise the white laundry of the soldiers fluttered in the breeze. I thought of a famous tanka by the Empress Jitō, found in the first volume of *Manyōshū*:

> Spring having passed by,
> Summer seems to have come at last.
> White
> Are the robes hung to dry
> Upon sacred Mount Kagu.

Adaptation accomplished?

THE JULY MORNING SKY as usual was clear. If there had been rain in the night it had stopped, as it generally did, by dawn, leaving a shimmering field stretched out to the southeast. As I went around and around on the dirt path I heard from within the verdant coppice numerous unidentified birds, whispering in charming tones. Once two butterflies tumbled close to me, and as I slowly resumed walking they sported now ahead of me, now behind, as if having a game with me. They floated on the gentle breeze that blew across the compound.

> Summer breeze
> Blows soothingly;
> In it,
> Gradually,
> I grow more submissive.

Ants, praying mantises, grasshoppers, toads, all manner of small creatures entered through the fencing. I became unwittingly attracted to these fleeting life forms. Soon I was

writing a tanka about each of them and growing to love them.
Especially the praying mantis.

> Facing me,
> Sicklelike forelimbs thrown up in front –
> Praying mantis.
> Bulging eyeballs,
> Black and lovable.

If I only opened my eyes I was free to see around me such dear
objects of delight as a dew-studded web across the grass, or the
faintest pulsation of a butterfly that had just alighted. And if
I were responsive, these were constantly ready to fire me to
poetic composition. I came to realize that if I observed subjects
carefully I could, as it were, simply bring forth the tanka that
grew within me one by one.

The garden afforded other visual stimuli. A wide variety of
flowers and vegetables, planted by other internees, were growing visibly day by day in response to careful tending. (Some
vegetables, welcome supplements to the scant portions of our
meals, were already appearing on the dinner table.) A particularly beautiful section of flowerbed was the handiwork of a
young friend of mine, who was very proud of his gardening
skill. He was cultivating morning glories, cosmos, asters, nas-
turtiums, and other varieties.

He had given me a single morning glory seedling, which I
had planted in an empty tobacco tin. I watered it morning and
evening and moved it several times a day so that it would
spend as long as possible in the sun. Despite my care its growth
was slow; I despaired of ever seeing it bloom. But later, in early
autumn, it was to push out one tiny bud. I was overjoyed. On
the third morning I awoke to the sight of a crimson bloom. I
called the other men over to see it, and we rejoiced together.
The blossoming was sensed as some sort of triumph. Before the

first bloom had withered a second bud appeared, and it too blossomed in a few days' time. The plant thus yielded a few more blooms one by one, but these were progressively smaller. Finally the morning came on which I saw the fifth and final bloom. No new bud had appeared to presage a sixth. I thought back over the joy that this plant's triumph over less than ideal growing conditions had brought me; I felt strongly that no matter what the particular interest, something that can sustain the emotions is a good thing.

There was in the camp a young pianist named Goromaru. In late July, through an introduction by a mutual friend, it was arranged that I would receive instruction from him. I was happy at the prospect of adding a pleasant practice session to my day. At first my fingers were stiff and refused to move as I wanted them to. But the kind youth gently took them in his and guided them until they gradually became flexible and capable of rapid movement. After much eager practice, I knew by heart one song of some three minutes' duration, 'Kōjō no Tsuki' ('Moonlight upon Castle Ruins'). Pleased with my meagre accomplishment, I continued to go to the recreation hall to play the tune to help while away the time.

Some others had started making many interesting things out of scraps of wood. The Japanese are generally skilful at working with their hands and derive much satisfaction from it. There must be other people who, like me, treasure to this day the elaborately carved picture frames made at that time. What superb mementos! Though over thirty years have passed, the well-wrought frame that I have still speaks silently of the life at Angler.

About this time the office next door to that of the camp leader was converted into a canteen. Following the regulations regarding prisoners of war, coupons were issued once a month. The money they represented was deducted from the funds that had been taken from us upon our arrival. Those who had come to the camp with no money were still issued coupons, though doubtless fewer than they would have liked. The coupons bought us whatever the store offered – tobacco, gum, candy, chocolate, soap, notebooks, and an assortment of daily needs.

This summer too, white wild roses bloomed at the base of the fence. One evening I stood by these sweetly perfumed blooms and looked at the moon. A famous tanka by Abe no Nakamaro, found in the ninth volume of *Kokinshū*, came to mind. The poet was a Japanese courtier, sent by the Emperor to the Chinese court during the early Heian period. Delicately expressed in his tanka was his longing for home. He had written:

> Sky.
> If I turn around and look,
> This moon seems to be the same one
> As that of Mount Mikasa
> Of Kasuga.

The shrill whirring of a cicada interrupted my thoughts. 'How strange a sound,' I thought. As I listened, another and then another joined in the chorus. In a minute the piercing noise was like a single violent force, boring into me like a drill. It penetrated ever deeper and deeper until I felt as though I were being constricted. At the point when it became nearly unbearable, the low cooing of wild pigeons broke into the performance and released me.

That night, after lights out, when the voices had gradually subsided, I fell victim to my thoughts. Again the familiar voice of many earlier nights started up accusingly: 'Just how long do you intend to remain in this camp? You're rather enjoying yourself, engaging in leisure pursuits all day, aren't you?' I felt that a judgment was being passed upon me – 'You have no intention of leaving this place!' – and I acquiesced. I could not help but suspect that they could not have kept me there as they had without, in some sense, my compliance: my mind had complied with my imprisonment because the very experience of that imprisonment had worked insidiously to convince me that I was somehow guilty. I resolved to do something, as soon as possible, to conquer this mental state.

Decision to leave

ON A SMALL HILL to the northeast the graves of seven German soldiers lay hidden beneath tall grass. I first learned that they were there on the day we were taken to clear them. Under a burning midsummer sun, five of us set out accompanied by two guards. We went out through those gates I had first come through fully a year before, in August 1942. Once outside, I paused for a moment to look up at the tall gateway. Already my cares seemed to have lifted. But as we steadily drew away from the gates, I kept turning to glance back at them.

German soldiers had been imprisoned at Angler earlier in the war. On an especially dark night, a group of them had dared an escape. But the attempt had ended in some of their number being shot dead by guards. Detained like them at Angler, we naturally felt sympathy. Having cleared away the overgrowth, we gathered the daisies of the fields and laid them on the graves.

When I had arrived at Angler the previous year and was making the rounds to see who had preceded me there, I had been heartily welcomed by one who shook my hand firmly and

said, 'Nakano, how good to see you! Japan shall win the war
for sure, you know!' It was S., a friend from Woodfibre. He lay
confined to bed with a chronic stomach ailment. When I came
to leave the camp some fourteen months later, S. tried his best
to stop me. He himself died there the following year. When I
heard that he had been buried in that bleak spot next to the
seven German soldiers, I felt deep pity – he had died without
ever having escaped the sorry environment of the internment
camp.

   With the sun slipping down in the western sky, evening had
begun to encroach upon the daylit hills of Angler. Against the
wire fence, the white tufts of tall grass gone to seed swayed in
a faint breeze. A lone quail took small hops through the mesh
of the fencing. The Japanese army-style drill usually took place
exactly then, in the inspiring setting of nature in the evening
sun. The drill was led by the onetime soldier who had had us
crop our hair very short before leaving the Immigration Building jail at Vancouver. The display brought to mind the well-
ordered ranks of the splendid Japanese imperial army of the
Meiji era, of my childhood. At the beginning and the end, the
participants stood at attention facing in the direction of Japan,
then bowed deeply from the waist. Just as the drill was completed, the sun dropped below the horizon, and dusk hurried
onto the scene.

> Army training.
> Perfectly synchronized
> Young men –
> Who know not real battle,
> Here in the internment camp.

   Because it was wartime and we Japanese were the enemy,
albeit securely imprisoned, it seemed strange that Japanese
army-style training had been allowed that summer. It had

made me wonder if the Allies had not already foreseen victory. I had long since begun to suspect the weekly news reported by the committee member assigned to the task: it seemed that the reports, since the beginning, habitually had understated Japan's losses and had overstated those of the United States. But I had kept my suspicions to myself. Likely others too had had such suspicions but had likewise not voiced them. It was difficult to give up my belief in Japan's eventual victory, the more so since it had not been a rational belief, but rather one born of the love I, as a Japanese national, still felt for my fatherland. But now, if my suspicions about the actual progress of the war were correct, it was much more urgent that I leave the camp.

About the time when the days were getting perceptibly shorter, we heard something of the latest war news, something it would have been difficult to disguise. On the European front, Allied forces had conducted in July and August the Sicilian campaign, which was to bring about the fall of Mussolini.

In early November, having admitted to myself the utter hopelessness of remaining at Angler, I applied to leave. I had then to reckon with M., an old man whom I had first met in the Immigration Building jail. He had chanced to learn of my move and had awaited an opportune moment, when many of us were out walking in the compound. There, before surprised faces, he launched into a severe tongue lashing. He said sharply to me: 'So you are going to leave here and work for Canada in wartime, are you? I suppose you don't know that that will aid the war effort against Japan. Still, I know a traitor to Japan when I see one!' Nor did he stop there. He heaped curses upon me for an interminable several minutes. Many years later I heard that he had eventually been moved to a smaller camp at Moose Jaw as one of the remaining internees, the true *gambariya* diehards. He was one of a number of such men who died without ever having left internment.

Since *gambariya* like M. numbered in the hundreds at
Angler, their views won the ascendancy. Consequently the
many younger men who wanted to take work and thus leave
the camp were intimidated and wavered in their intentions.
Their hesitation made me feel deep regret at the waste of their
young lives. They had clearly become quite weary of the camp
life. During the day there were some chores they had to do.
And when those were done they could engage in a wide range
of recreational activities. But they really were left with too
much leisure time. Moreover, when night came the high
spirits of the day vanished, and the men fell silent.

On rare occasions some jollity lasted after dark. One September evening, three youths sat on a bed near mine and
joined their voices in singing the popular 'Shanhai Musume.'
Because they sang so well we shouted for an encore, but to no
avail. The moment past, the youths were subdued, and looked
exceedingly pitiable. Hours after lights out, I continued to
think of them. I heard the regular footfalls of the night guard
approach from the distance and then recede. From below my
window came the chirping of crickets, to lull me to sleep.

Each day the coppice beyond the fence added more golds,
reds, and browns to its display. Before I realized it we were
into the season when cold winds penetrated the flesh, and wild
geese flew past daily on the trip south. The wild flowers that
had bloomed extravagantly just days before, and the flowers
and vegetables of the garden, succumbed to frost. They lay
with muted colour, dying. A desolation spread imperceptibly
within the compound.

In the lull of the spirit that invariably descended upon me
after the evening meal, I went off alone for my walk along the
footpath. One evening I spotted a line of wild geese flying into
the sunset, honking noisily as it went. I watched as the line
turned into a perfect V, then continued to track the flight for a
long time. At last the geese disappeared into the distant sunset.

But my thoughts continued to trail after them, and beyond to my dear ones in faraway British Columbia.

Still in reverie, I looked about me and saw a number of the other men walking mutely about the compound. They gazed upon the soon-to-set sun as though to detain it. A good distance ahead of me a youth walked alone, the red circle on his back burning in the intense light of the fiery orb. As he moved, it looked as though blood from a large wound were soaking his shirt.

The quiet Nisei youth who had the bunk above me talked that evening of many things. That morning he had received a letter from his girlfriend, who had been evacuated to Greenwood. Her letters seemed always to make him melancholy. He told me once again that he and she were waiting for the war to end so that they could get married. For this youth and for the countless others like him, whose promising futures lay far from the camp, I prayed that the war would be over even a day sooner.

The Department of Labour had sent representatives to Angler with offers of various employment opportunities for those who wished to resume a normal life in Canada. In the severe cold of February earlier that year, 1943, about thirty internees, mainly young Nisei but also a handful of older Issei, in order to get out of the camp had taken jobs in the bush of Neys, Ontario. Their move had not been common knowledge at the time, but, much later, reports of their hardships had come as a warning to us back at the camp. I therefore wanted to leave in the warm weather and had been waiting for a suitable job. Meanwhile the situation in the camp had been very delicate indeed. The *gambariya* were ever vigilant for traitors to their cause. The government, they said, had been wrong to uproot them from their lives. It had forced them from their homes, had split up their families, and had confiscated their property and possessions, only to leave them to be stolen or vandalized, or to auction them off. Now that same government would have to host them for a while. No one was to leave the camp until the day when a victorious Japan would force the Canadian government to make full restitution to the ill-treated Japanese Canadian civilians. Some of these *gambariya* planned to return then to Japan; others would re-establish themselves here. In the midst of a consensus in support of *gambariya* convictions, no doubt it was difficult to make arrangements surreptitiously to leave. But some had managed this, for, as I learned later, some job opportunities had been made available since early 1943, and had been accepted. It was probably because I generally kept to myself that I, for one, did not hear of them until they were fully common knowledge.

It was now late October. I began to put in order the tanka, haiku, diary entries, and prose jottings that had accumulated over the months I had been at Angler, in order that I should be ready to leave at any time. So far no one knew that I had decided to leave sometime soon. I continued to attend the meetings of the haiku club, which had now been in existence for over a year. The sorrow of soon parting from my haiku friends troubled me already.

Secret arrangements for departure

IT WAS NOW the second week of November. When I looked back, over fourteen long months had passed since I had been sent to the camp from Vancouver. When one said 'fourteen months,' it did not seem such a long time. But those fourteen months in the internment camp, with the world outside at war, had been a unique experience. The world situation had changed greatly. In the Pacific theatre and on the European front, a life-and-death struggle had doubtless repeated itself daily. Meanwhile, in the utterly isolated camp, there had been in daily operation a different reality, one in which it seemed that time had slowed nearly to a stop. Yet there I had undergone an unexpected trial, recording a personal history of at times barely endurable anxiety; from that trial I emerged a changed man.

Having made my decision to leave, I had applied to do so in such a way as I hoped would elude public notice. With something to look forward to, I now found that the days sped by. Angler was already showing signs of winter; the war news we heard was as bleak as the surroundings. Since October, U.S. forces had been trying to take Bougainville Island, the most important base of the Solomon Islands sector in the South Pacific. A furious battle thus raged there by sea, by land, and by air. In the central Pacific, successive landings by parties of American marines had resulted in the taking of the Gilbert Islands base. These moves had broken Japan's defence line and thereby had reduced greatly her control of Pacific waters.

Camp life continued with no visible change. One afternoon, for the first time in months, I went to the station to pick up the coal shipment. By the time we had finished loading the truck, the rails of the transcontinental railroad were carmine in the final rays of the setting sun. They burned their route into the distance, plunging through the rocky terrain and forests, destined for the more populous region of southern Ontario. What a barren and soundless landscape – until the silence was shattered by the clanging of the freight cars pulling out of the station.

Well before the first stars had begun to wink, the bright lamps were turned on. The evening chill made a sudden invasion. In the dimly lit dormitory, I made my way to bed, where I read squinty-eyed until lights out at ten. Then, as I looked out the window, it seemed that everything beyond the fence was sound asleep in the darkness. I tried to sleep but was kept awake by such questions as, 'What will happen henceforth in the war?' and, 'What course will world events take at the war's end?' Having fallen into circumstances that forced me to consider large questions for the first time, I did not know what to make of the world situation, or of humanity, or even of the self I had become. I had searched for answers but had not found any that were satisfactory. Only that favourite verse of Isaiah 40:31 lingered in my mind:

They that wait upon the Lord shall renew their strength; they shall mount up with wings as eagles; they shall run, and not be weary; and they shall walk, and not faint.

On November 14, a couple of weeks after submitting my application to go to Toronto to work for Canada Packers, I was told that Ottawa had approved it. My emotions upon hearing the news were mixed. I was glad, certainly, but also apprehensive. Toronto was a place I had never seen, I knew no one there, and I was now to go there alone, to a job about which I knew next to nothing. In Woodfibre's Japanese community, in the road camps, and in the internment camp, it had not mattered that I spoke so little English. Now this too was a problem.

The next night, my last in the camp, after bidding quick farewells to those closest to me, I went to bed and lay awake with a head full of visions bred of excitement. After only a short sleep, I awoke while the stars were still twinkling. Soon I was up and busy, preparing to leave. I had few possessions to pack. As I packed my accumulated writings, I tried not to think of the possibility that they might be confiscated at the exit. As it turned out, I need not have worried. They easily passed a hasty routine inspection.

On that November 16, 1943, two others were leaving for Toronto, though for different jobs from mine. Two soldiers were escorting us to the station. As we neared the gates, five scowling *gambariya* appeared from nowhere and stalked towards us. Fear of an attack gripped my heart. But, held at bay by the presence of the guards, the send-off party dared not touch us. Shielded from the guards by the language barrier, however, they clearly felt no compunction to restrain their tongues. The *gambariya* jeered at us furiously, a long stream of names and curses. The old man M., who just the week before had shamed me publicly, would not let this opportunity pass. He went so far as to spit at us. The walk to the gates seemed long indeed, but before we knew it we had slipped out, quietly and effortlessly. Then I was walking along the roadway I had first travelled over fourteen months before – now for the last time, headed for the station, and beyond it, freedom. How many times did I turn to look back at the grim gates, the barbed wire fences, the high watchtowers, the bleak compound.

As we arrived, the Toronto-bound train was just pulling into the station, its whistle summoning us. No one got off the train, and we three were the only ones to board. A small quantity of freight was quickly unloaded. We bade a hasty farewell to our guards. The train started up again. I gave a great sigh of relief. In that moment I felt that I had somehow been given a new start. I was forever cut off from all that had been before Angler. With the war not yet over, I did not even try to guess what fate held in store for me next. Besides, that did not seem to matter much at the moment. I felt better able to cope with whatever the future held.

The small station had an incongruously large signboard bearing big orange letters spelling out 'Angler.' As the train pulled away, my eyes stayed fixed upon those letters. Yet in the distance I thought I could just make out the camp, where my eight hundred brothers were still captive. 'Oh Angler, sayonara!' I cried out in a broken voice.

Epilogue: Toronto and a fresh start

I THOUGHT of how the train was taking me farther from my loved ones in British Columbia, yet bringing me closer to them in that now I could work for our reunion: I had been told that the government would move my family from Greenwood as soon as I was established in my job and had found appropriate housing for them. With this to look forward to, I relaxed into my seat and enjoyed the view. I had the sense of leaving the past far behind, as my thoughts and emotions raced ahead of the speeding train. The only shadow that crossed my mind came momentarily as I thought of the hundreds still left behind.

On November 17, 1943, at 10 am, I got off the train at Union Station in Toronto. I had been told that a Canada Packers representative would be there to meet me. Accordingly, a gentleman now approached me, introduced himself and shook my hand, took my bags, and led me off to the coffee shop for a little refreshment. Once in his car, we did not proceed directly to Somerville Hostel at Dundas Street West and the old Highway 27. (This residence, as I later learned, had been provided for Japanese workers by Canada Packers.)

Instead my kindly escort took me on a tour of the waterfront at Sunnyside, gratifying indeed after a long confinement. The freighters on the lake gave me a sense of what a great metropolis Toronto was. I felt that I had come to a good place.

At the residence, I was surprised to see more than thirty Japanese men, most of whom I recognized as those who had left Angler for work in Neys. I was glad to be in the company of so many who spoke Japanese.

For the several weeks I was at the residence, I was taken with the others by truck to and from work each day. Though the hours were long, the work was not difficult, and we were treated very well. Meanwhile I found a place that would house my family. I made ready to receive Yukie and Toshimi at any time. On December 18, 1943, after twenty-one months apart, we were reunited.

> Reunited.
> Now to join in recompense
> With the harmonious group at table –
> Narcissi's
> Strong scent.

The only requirement upon us Japanese was that we report once a month at the RCMP office on Adelaide Street East, to keep the authorities up to date on our residence and employment. I had been lucky to get into Toronto while the ban on Japanese entering the city was relaxed. And, to look at things in the most positive way, had I not been sent to Angler I would certainly not have come to the east so soon, if at all. In 1944 and in the next few years, when the government was ordering the Japanese to go east or go to Japan, many feared coming east because of reports of harsh climate and lack of job

OPPOSITE: A reunited family in Toronto

prospects. Besides, there was no reason for them to expect less racial prejudice here than on the west coast. Thus thousands chose to go to Japan.

But I was here in Toronto. And having no hope of recovering what I had had to leave behind in Woodfibre, I intended to make a fresh start. I worked hard at Canada Packers, with much the same spirit as that with which I had set to work as an immigrant over twenty years before. When Japan acknowledged defeat on August 15, 1945, I was torn with grief. But I was thankful that the war was over at long last.

My family was now truly getting on with life in Toronto. Toshimi was growing up happily in the only country she knew as home. Thus in a few years, Yukie and I, who since coming to Toronto had been seriously considering taking Canadian citizenship, made up our minds. On December 8, 1948, we became Canadians, like our daughter. It was with mixed feelings that I renounced my beloved fatherland.

I worked a quarter-century at Canada Packers, until my retirement in 1968. This is remarkable to me when I recall that when I first went there in 1943 I did not dream that I would stay so long.

Now I wonder how many have ever heard of the internment camp at Angler, Ontario. Likely few who were there still speak of it. But all who were there remember the part it played in the second world war evacuation of Japanese Canadians.

TAKEO NAKANO was to continue the pursuit of tanka composition to which he had devoted so much time and effort during
his internment. In 1964, years after the events of the foregoing
account, a tanka he had written was one of twelve chosen
from 46,886 entries in the annual Imperial Poetry Contest.
(His was the first successful Canadian entry in the contest's
history.) He went to Tokyo to be present at the recitation of
the winning poems before Emperor Hirohito and Empress
Nagako. Takeo had written:

> As final resting place,
> Canada is chosen.
> On citizenship paper,
> Signing
> Hand trembles.

LEATRICE NAKANO

Afterword

Afterword

W. PETER WARD

TAKEO NAKANO was born in 1903 in the farming village of Takatsuka, which is part of the town of Shiida in Fukuoka-ken, on the island of Kyushu, Japan. He was the second of five surviving children, all of them male. His parents were rice farmers. They owned a plot of land just large enough to support the family and his paternal grandparents, who once had worked the farm themselves but since had retired to live with their eldest son. His maternal grandparents were chandlers in a nearby farming village. Only a minority of the villagers owned farms, most of them being sharecroppers who rented from one of the few substantial landowners in the district. Consequently, while far from rich the Nakanos were comparatively well off. As small landholders they could enjoy the greater security, status, wealth, and independence of minor proprietorship.

One indication of this relative advantage was the family's superior education. Takeo's father had completed public schooling in the late nineteenth century, an achievement which set him apart from most contemporaries of his social class. In this respect the son was to surpass the father. Takeo graduated from an agricultural high school in his home prefecture at the age of sixteen at a time when only one Japanese child in six would proceed beyond the first phase of secondary schooling and only one in ten would enter, let alone graduate from, a higher vocational school.[1]

The cultural life of the Nakano family also included a deep interest in poetry. Takeo's father was a haiku poet of local reputation and from him, at the age of fifteen, Takeo took his earliest literary instruction. His elder brother and two younger brothers became haiku poets in turn and they, too, earned some local recognition. That a family of rice farmers in early twentieth century Japan should have well-developed literary tastes was by no means exceptional, for poetry was a highly valued Japanese cultural tradition. By the late nineteenth century the writing of verse, once the exclusive pastime of Japanese social and cultural elites, had become increasingly popular. Nonetheless, in the context of their village, the Nakanos were better educated and more deeply immersed in poetic traditions than most of their neighbours.

Takeo left home for Canada in 1920 while still in his midteens. As a second son he had no prospect of inheritance, for land in Japan normally passed to the eldest son, who supported his mother and father in return: this had been the case with Takeo's own parents. Should the family farm have been divided amongst him and his brothers, the fragments would have been too small to support them and the families they would one day acquire. Takeo thus came to British Columbia to work on his uncle's small berry farm near Hammond. His initial hope, soon abandoned, was to save enough for the purchase of a farm in Canada. When experience altered his goals, he planned to stay on the west coast until he could afford a farm in Japan. After two years, however, his uncle could no longer employ him. He then found a job at the pulp mill in Woodfibre, just north of Vancouver on the west coast of Howe Sound. There he worked as a labourer for the next twenty years. He returned to Japan only once, in 1930, to visit his family and marry. Three years later his first child, a daughter, was born. Despite the lengthening years he spent in Canada, Takeo never entirely relinquished his wish to go back to Japan. As long as he lived in British Columbia he remained something of a sojourner. But as with thousands of other young Japanese who left home to seek economic opportunity abroad, time and circumstance changed his aspirations. Marriage and the birth of a child brought new attachments to Canada and, while dreams of return to Japan did not vanish, they gradually began to recede.

In Woodfibre Takeo was relatively isolated from the province's Japanese community. Though near Vancouver, Woodfibre could be reached only by boat; consequently his social and cultural life was largely confined to the pulp town where he lived. He acted as secretary to the local affiliate of a Japanese citizens' group in Vancouver – it maintained a library in the city, to which he had access – but he otherwise had few ties with the wider immigrant society. During these years his literary activity was slight. From time to time he wrote poetry and short articles for publication in Japanese Canadian periodicals. But his literary energies did not gather strength until after the outbreak of war. Then, when he was nearly forty, under the disruption and deprivation of the evacuation, his poetic gifts became manifest. The experiences which led to this development, as well as some of its fruits, are recorded in these reminiscences.

Tanka, the poetic mode in which Takeo preferred to write, had been the dominant verse form in Japanese literature for over a millennium. The 'short poem,' its name in translation, consists of thirty-one syllables arranged in five lines, the first and third being five and the others seven syllables long.* Its origins lay in the late seventh century when a literary culture began to emerge from the more primitive song and poetry of the folk culture of ancient Japan and from that time onward it remained 'the formal constant of the Japanese tradition.'[2] In the classical period (784-1350) it was the poetic form most commonly employed in court society, the expression of an aristocratic culture which highly valued the writing of verse. Tanka are to be found in large numbers in the earliest collections of Japanese poetry as well as in the twenty-one imperial anthologies gathered together between the tenth and fifteenth centuries. This tradition of imperial patronage continues today in the Emperor's annual poetry contest, held during the new year season. With the spread of literacy in Japan during the nineteenth century, the writing of poetry became more popular, tanka remaining the preferred form of expression. Poetry groups were established in many communities and poetry competitions came to be regular events. (Japanese immigrants in British Columbia occasionally established such groups after 1900 too, their compositions often being published in the province's Japanese-language newspapers.) Thus, by the twentieth century the writing of poetry had become a common Japanese pastime and tanka the preferred poetic mode. Its shortness made it an intensive verse form and, despite the constraints of its rigid formal structure, in the hands of generations of Japanese poets it had become a rich and supple means of expression. It seems particularly well suited to introspection, detailed observation, and personal reflection – those tasks for which Takeo employed it – though over the centuries it has sustained a broad range of themes.

* The tanka in this reminiscence have been translated in such a way as to preserve their meaning and phrasing but not their syllabic structure.

The vicissitudes of wartime brought Takeo to Toronto, where he settled permanently when peace returned. He and his wife became Canadian citizens in 1948 and in the following year a second daughter was born to them. He began an intensive study of the writing of tanka through correspondence, first with a club in Seattle and then with the celebrated Chōōn sha Tanka Club in Kamakura, Japan. In 1964 he was one of twelve winners in Japan's annual Imperial Poetry Contest, which in that year attracted close to 47,000 entrants. Soon after he founded a tanka club in Toronto to which he still gives instruction. He published a volume of his prose and poetry entitled *Sensei* ('Oath of Citizenship') in Japan in 1969 and since then has had many of his tanka published in anthologies on both sides of the Pacific. Retired since 1968, he has continued to devote himself to writing, some of his most recent works being commemorative poems.

Takeo's reminiscences are unique in both the English- and the Japanese-language literature on Canada's Japanese community. They are the only available, substantial account of the experiences and reflections of an Issei, or first-generation immigrant from Japan. In particular they provide the clearest glimpse we have of Japanese loyalism and internment camp life during the second world war. Those detained at Angler had been imprisoned for disobeying evacuation orders, but not all had done so for the same reasons. Many were loyal to Japan and their refusal to co-operate was a political act prompted by a mixture of motives: sympathy for the enemy, belief in his ultimate victory, and opposition to a government policy regarded as unjust. Others like Takeo were ambivalent; whatever their loyalties, they had made no overt political gestures. Instead they had balked at some specific requirement of the evacuation process and had been jailed for their recalcitrance. In camp the mingling of these two groups created an intensely political atmosphere, one which constantly fed on accumulated grievances, fragments of war news, rumour, and idle speculation. The Japanese loyalists were more numerous, outspoken, and articulate than others in the camp, and they had an unambiguous cause to uphold. Theirs was a coercive mentality, which seems to have silenced most dissenting opinion at Angler. The strength of the loyalist consensus is revealed by the furtiveness required of those who left the camp to accept work from Canadian authorities. Thus, while far from a microcosm of the Japanese immigrant community, those confined at Angler represented two divergent responses to tensions which war created within the minority society. Only a small proportion of all Japanese Canadians felt unswerving loyalty to Japan. Like Takeo, most were ultimately torn between two allegiances. But at Angler the balance tipped in the other direction. There the loyalists were dominant.

As Takeo was only one of thousands of immigrants to Canada from Japan, his personal history should be set against that of the Japanese community as a whole. Between the mid-1890s and the outbreak of the second world war, almost 5,000,000 immigrants entered Canada. Of them 39,000 came from Japan, well under one per cent of the incoming population. While the first Japanese set foot in Canada in 1877, the great majority arrived during the decade and a half before the first world war, most of them in two great waves of 11,000 each in 1899-1900 and 1906-7. Of course not all these migrants remained permanently in Canada. Many of the earlier arrivals quickly left for the United States. Others stayed for varying lengths of time and then returned to Japan. Consequently the Japanese population of Canada grew rather more slowly than these figures suggest. The community consisted of fewer than 5000 souls in 1901, when it was first recognized on the federal census, and over the next thirty years it grew to 23,000, a size it more or less maintained into the 1950s. Until 1942, over 95 per cent of the Japanese in Canada lived in British Columbia, where they were heavily concentrated in Vancouver and the neighbouring Fraser River delta.[3]

From a demographic perspective, the Japanese migration can be divided into two distinct phases. The first, which lasted until about 1910, was dominated by the entry of adult males, most of them between the ages of fifteen and thirty years. By and large they came from rural village backgrounds and commonly had been farmers, fishermen, or labourers before embarkation. For the most part they came to Canada with no intention of permanent settlement. Bound by family and cultural ties to their native land, yet impelled by population pressures and rural poverty at home, they had migrated to seek their fortune abroad with the expectation of some day returning to Japan. Many must have realized their material aspirations in some measure. In the later 1930s, one estimate suggested that between 12,000 and 13,000 Japanese had repatriated themselves, though with what degree of financial security we have no way of knowing.[4] Temporary residence, or sojourning, thus characterized the first phase of Japanese immigration to Canada. It introduced to British Columbia a population that was overwhelmingly male and transient.[5]

From the outset, however, some Japanese came intending to make Canada their home, and presumably their numbers increased over time. Many also arrived planning to return to Japan, but of necessity settled permanently in Canada. The shift from temporary to permanent migration began just before the first world war and became the dominant characteristic of the second phase of Japanese immigration. This change was marked by the preponderance of young women in the immigrant population: after 1910 women constituted more than half of all arrivals from Japan, their average age being about twenty-five years. Behind this upsurge in female migration lay the 'picture bride' system of proxy marriage, which united men in Canada with wives in Japan they often had never seen. The arrival of women, marriage, and family formation were thus both portents and causes of the new impulse toward permanent settlement. The fruit of these unions were the Nisei, the second generation, born in Canada, raised as Canadians, and for the most part unfamiliar with things Japanese. Numbering over 13,000 by 1941,[6] they were caught between two distinctively different cultures, an experience shared in one way or another by thousands of children born of immigrants in Canada during the nineteenth and twentieth centuries.

Upon arrival, the Japanese entered the lowest strata of the British Columbian labour force. With skills best adapted to the rural village economy of a society based upon fishing and wet rice agriculture, they had little more to offer than their labour. The one exception was in the fishing industry, to which some brought skills and knowledge; as a result, the Japanese came to be concentrated in that industry at the end of the nineteenth century. Thereafter they became the predominant influence in the west coast fisheries and remained so until the 1920s when, under strong pressure from white fishermen, the federal government reduced the number of licences given to those of Japanese ancestry. On the whole, however, the immigrants took such work as they could find, frequently in the saw and pulp mills of the province. After 1900 mixed farming and soft fruit farming attracted increasing numbers. Others found work in the commercial and service sectors, often within the confines of the minority community itself. Over the years, outward and upward mobility marked their employment patterns. But these processes had little more than begun when war interrupted them. On the eve of Pearl Harbor most Japanese still worked in a few occupations where their hours were long, their work arduous, their pay modest, and their status low.[7]

While they had little difficulty finding work in British Columbia, Japanese immigrants were only marginally integrated into the local society. By and large they clung together in communities which stood apart. They tended to live in their own small enclaves: Powell Street in Vancouver, the nearby fishing village of Steveston, and many other scattered, less populous settlements. Cultural ties, housing costs, restrictive covenants, and racial prejudice all reinforced these residential boundaries, which persisted until the wartime dispersal. The immigrants also established their own community institutions in order to meet the social, economic, cultural, philanthropic, and political needs of a small minority isolated within an unsympathetic host society. Newspapers, trade unions, businessmen's organizations, educational societies, and religious associations exclusive to the Japanese were established within the immigrant community by the early twentieth century, many of them patterned on Japanese models while others were largely North American in origin. Perhaps most interesting of all, some transplanted Japanese institutions borrowed freely from their Canadian counterparts in order to adapt more successfully to the new world environment. Buddhist temples, for example, imitated the worship and Sunday school programs of the Christian church in Canada, even to the point of adapting Christian hymns for Buddhist purposes.[8] Whatever their form, however, these organizations were the preserve of the Japanese community. While racial integration occurred to some extent in the workplace, and while Christian missionaries built a slender bridge between newcomers and their hosts, essentially the Japanese immigrant community remained a self-contained entity within west coast society.

While the Japanese in British Columbia were assimilated only to a limited extent, their acculturation was rather more rapid. Far more quickly than other Asians, they absorbed the language, customs, and values of western Canadian society. This process moved slowest among the Issei, its progress retarded by their trans-Pacific ties, the sojourner mentality, and the inherent difficulties adults face when learning new cultural responses. It also proceeded more slowly among women than men, for domestic life sheltered them from the need to adopt the new culture and they could enjoy reasonably full social lives within the boundaries of the minority community. Men, on the other hand, tended to encounter the world of whites more often and consequently came gradually to bear something of its imprint. Among the Nisei, acculturation progressed much more quickly. Born and raised in Canada, they attended local schools, played ball in community parks, and went to the movies at neighbourhood theatres. While many parents strove hard to instil a sense of 'Japaneseness' in their children – the thousands who attended Japanese-language schools on Saturday mornings testified to these aspirations – the force of North American popular culture proved irresistible. Culturally speaking, the Nisei became Canadians. For many, a yawning gap stood between them and their parents.

Whatever the extent of Japanese acculturation, however, the barriers of racism lay across the path to assimilation. White society in British Columbia was emphatically anti-Oriental.[9] When the first Japanese arrived in the province they encountered a community already divided by sharp racial cleavages. Chinese immigrants had preceded them by two decades and in the intervening years white society had developed a strong antipathy towards Asians in general. Thus the Japanese met hostility from the moment of their arrival, and thereafter bore the burden of this racist legacy. In the eyes of west coast whites these newcomers, like their predecessors, appeared aggressive, unfairly competitive, disloyal, and unassimilable. They seemed a threat to the cultural and economic destiny of the white community and on the basis of these assumptions the host society constructed an elaborate discriminatory apparatus. During the late nineteenth century the existing legal disabilities of the Chinese were extended to the Japanese. First, franchise laws denied them the vote and thus rendered them politically impotent. Further measures limited their employment opportunities and prevented their purchase of crown lands; diplomatic accords between Japan and Canada restricted their immigration; sporadic attempts were made to segregate Asian children in some provincial schools. These goals were not invariably met. But government restrictions did impose substantial burdens on all Asians in British Columbia, the Japanese included.

Acts of parliament, of legislatures, and of municipal councils, however, scarcely reveal the texture of race relations in British Columbia, for such policies were the outgrowth of assumptions, beliefs, and prejudices about Asians which were widely held in white society. Fundamentally west coast racism was a popular phenomenon. From the late 1850s, when the first Chinese immigrants arrived, anti-Orientalism was endemic on the west coast. Not all whites were racist, nor were their prejudices always aroused. But the anti-Oriental consensus was extremely broad and enduring. Before the Pacific war it dominated all public discussion of matters related to Asian Canadians and it encountered virtually no contradiction. At various times special interest groups, notably the labour movement, became the primary spokesmen of the anti-Oriental crusade. On other occasions popular racism created its own organizations to articulate public feelings. From time to time outspoken politicians also led opinion. Outbreaks of popular racism, however, were always episodic: intermittent peaks of sharp hostility were followed by long intervals of quiescence. A wide range of incidents could prompt these outbursts: sudden increases in Asian immigration, economic conflict, and during the 1930s Japan's expansionist actions in Asia. But whatever their immediate origins, and whoever their spokesmen, they all drew heavily on a deep reservoir of popular racial animus in the province.

Before the late 1930s five major anti-Oriental outbursts occurred in British Columbia. The first, in Victoria in 1878, was prompted by an increase in Chinese immigration and was led by an early provincial workingmen's organization. The second took place in Vancouver in 1886 and 1887 when white residents mounted a systematic campaign to prevent Chinese labourers from entering the burgeoning city; on one occasion a group of newly arrived Chinese labourers was driven out of town by mob violence. A third occurred in Vancouver two decades later when sharp increases in Chinese and Japanese immigration suddenly introduced thousands of Asians to British Columbia. The consequences were an aroused public temper, a sustained popular outcry, and a major race riot in September 1907. In 1914 the fourth incident – an attempt by 376 Sikhs aboard the *Komagata Maru* to land in Vancouver in defiance of Canadian immigration law – prompted further protest, although in this instance violence was prevented when the Canadian government stood firm and the ship was escorted out to sea without landing most of its passengers. Finally, between 1919 and 1922 racism again welled up in the province. Farmers' organizations opposed Asian landholding, small businessmen mounted a drive against Asian retail merchants, and the sensationalist press launched a yellow peril campaign.

Most such attacks were made upon Asians regardless of their nationality, but following the turn of the century the Japanese gradually became the primary targets of white animosity. Among the various causes of this development, one predominates: Japan's growing military presence in Asia. After her victory over Russia in 1905 Japan seemed, in the eyes of an ever increasing number of whites in western North America, an aggressive power with a grand imperial design embracing the whole North Pacific basin. Throughout the inter-war years the Japanese in British Columbia lived in the shadow of these fears. Not only were they deemed unassimilable, aggressive, and an economic menace – traditional stereotypes commonly applied to all Asian immigrants – but also a potential military threat. Ostensibly loyal to an expansionist and militaristic Japan, they conjured up visions of espionage and fifth column activity. Needless to say such assumptions were groundless. At no time before or during the second world war was treachery ever discovered among the Japanese in Canada. Nevertheless the threat seemed real enough to many white British Columbians.

These convictions, largely quiescent before 1931, were roused by Japan's invasion of Manchuria that year. Over the next decade the image of Japanese militarism clouded popular impressions of the Japanese in British Columbia. In growing numbers whites suspected that the immigrant community harboured illegal immigrants and Japanese military officers who were infiltrating the province for subversive purposes. Japan's attack on China in the summer of 1937 prompted a new outbreak of hostility.[10] A second followed in the spring of 1940, this time in the anxious atmosphere of the early months of war. The final racial outburst, more intense, more widespread, and more alarmist than ever before, was touched off by Japan's sudden attack on Pearl Harbor on December 7, 1941.

The ensuing course of popular agitation and policy development can be summarized quite briefly. Immediately after the declaration of war the federal government arrested thirty-eight Japanese previously identified as possible security threats, closed Japanese-language cultural institutions, sequestered the west coast Japanese fishing fleet, and called for public calm. These measures did not quiet popular fears, however, and during the next few weeks strident demands came from the white community in British Columbia for all Japanese in the province to be interned. In mid-January, under continued pressure, the federal government announced a partial evacuation program whereby all enemy aliens would be moved from protected zones in British Columbia. The government also promised to create a labour corps which would enlist male Canadian citizens of Japanese ancestry who were of military age and place them on work projects outside the protected areas. These pledges mollified west coast opinion temporarily but in the end failed to contain it. After a short time came a hostile outburst more intense than any in the previous history of provincial race relations; it demanded the removal of all Japanese from coastal areas. In the face of such vehemence the federal government capitulated. On February 27 it announced to the public that all persons of Japanese ancestry would be evacuated from the protected areas of British Columbia.

During the next seven months the government forced over 21,000 to abandon their homes and relocate under federal supervision.[11] The British Columbia Security Commission, the federal agency created to carry out the evacuation, discharged its task methodically and systematically. As a first step it acquired the Hastings Park Exhibition Grounds in Vancouver for use as a shelter and clearing house for evacuees. The centre's first residents were Japanese from Vancouver Island and outlying coastal districts, those selected for initial removal. Housed in temporary quarters – hastily converted livestock pens – they were thrust rudely into the unsettling world of wartime dislocation. The Commission's task of finding destinations for the evacuees was complicated by federal desire for economy, which in turn made maximum Japanese self-sufficiency a goal, and by extensive white opposition to a Japanese presence in inland provincial towns. As a result most of the evacuees were sent to relatively isolated areas. First to go were some 2200 men – Takeo Nakano among them – who were placed in several interior road camps. A further 4000 were sent to work on sugar beet farms in southern Alberta and Manitoba. Some

12,000 – the majority – were dispatched to housing projects in the interior of the province, either to one of several renovated ghost towns in the Kootenay Lake and Slocan Valley districts or to a newly constructed camp at Tashme, east of Hope.

Throughout the first year of the Pacific war, the federal government interned an additional 758 Japanese. Aside from the thirty-eight who had been immediately arrested as threats to national security, most were imprisoned between March and November of 1942 for resisting evacuation orders. Many were members of the Nisei Mass Evacuation Group, an informal body of second-generation Japanese Canadians who opposed the evacuation policy.[12] After initial detention in the federal immigration hall on the Vancouver waterfront, the internees were sent to a prison camp at Angler, Ontario, near the town of Marathon on the north shore of Lake Superior. Because this was considered a disciplinary rather than a security measure, and because Ottawa wished to reduce the number of Japanese dependent on the state for support, the Security Commission encouraged prisoners to leave the camp for work in southern Ontario and, through the federal Department of Labour, arranged for job placement. In 1943, 300 internees departed, leaving a core of 425 obdurate protestors in detention where they remained until the end of the war.

In 1944 the King government, under opposition attack for its lack of a comprehensive policy on the Japanese problem, sought a permanent solution to the question.[13] Public opinion and political pressure strongly opposed the evacuees' return to their former homes. Yet the majority of Japanese were still housed in temporary locations. It was decided to force those then living in the interior of British Columbia – still two-thirds of the Japanese Canadian minority – to chose between resettlement east of the Rockies and repatriation to Japan. In the bitterness and confusion which followed, nearly 11,000 Japanese

– nationals, naturalized Canadians, and Canadian-born alike – opted to go to Japan. In the interior camps of British Columbia, over 80 per cent of the adults favoured repatriation: rejection of Canada was general. East of the Rockies, on the other hand, only 15 per cent wished to leave.[14] Subsequently two-thirds of those who had declared for repatriation changed their minds. The King government was adamant; arguing that the decision to leave was evidence of disloyalty to Canada (save among those who had repented before VJ day), it pursued its original course. In 1946, however, after a sustained campaign of opposition and a lengthy struggle in the courts, Japanese Canadian activists and liberal white sympathizers forced the government to yield. Ultimately only 4000 left Canada for Japan, all of them voluntarily. Of those who remained, the majority relocated on the prairies or in eastern Canada, where they found new homes and jobs and resumed normal lives. Thus by 1949 only 30 per cent of the 20,000 Japanese in Canada still lived in British Columbia. The pattern and structure of Japanese Canadian society had been altered permanently.

During the mid- and late-1940s, Canadian attitudes toward resident Asians in general, and the Japanese in particular, began to shift significantly. While racist opinion remained pervasive, liberal sentiments about race relations rapidly gained ascendancy. Since the early 1930s white spokesmen had occasionally called for fair treatment of the Japanese, but their cries had gone largely unheeded. It took the prospect of wholesale Japanese deportation to create a broader coalition of white humanitarians and civil rights activists with Japanese Canadian protestors in defence of minority group interests. After the Allied victory, wartime restrictions on the Japanese were relaxed, albeit gradually. The franchise was extended to adult citizens of Asian ancestry, the Chinese and East Indians in 1947 and the Japanese two years later. At the same time restrictive laws were repealed and soon legal discrimination against Asians in Canada was largely a thing of the past, though immigration from the Far East remained sharply curtailed until the 1960s.

Racism persisted after the war in its more quiet and subtle forms. Yet policy and attitude were greatly relaxed, perhaps surprisingly so when one considers the century-long history of white antipathy in British Columbia. One reason for this change was that, once dispersed, the Japanese no longer seemed the social and economic peril they had once appeared. Obviously, as well, Japan's defeat had eliminated all prospect of a military threat, either external or internal. Then, too, revelations of German and Japanese war atrocities cast racism into unprecedented disrepute throughout the western world, forcing opponents of Asians in Canada onto the defensive and ultimately into silence. Finally, decades of acculturation had begun to reveal their fruit. By the late 1940s the great majority of Japanese Canadians had been born and raised in Canada. Having absorbed the fundamental norms and values of the larger society about them they no longer were separated from whites by a wide cultural gulf. Consequently they aroused much less concern and antagonism than had their immigrant parents. In the process of becoming Canadian the Japanese had finally won a measure of acceptance.

1 H.D. Smith, *Japan's First Student Radicals* (Cambridge, Mass., 1972), 3
2 R.H. Brower and E. Miner, *Japanese Court Poetry* (Stanford, Calif., 1961), 11
3 K. Adachi, *The Enemy That Never Was: A History of the Japanese Canadians* (Toronto, 1976), Appendix I, Tables 1 and 3, 412-13

4 C.H. Young and H.R.Y. Reid, *The Japanese Canadians* (Toronto, 1938), 30

5 Young and Reid, *The Japanese Canadians*, 16-17

6 Adachi, *The Enemy That Never Was*, Appendix II, Table 5, 414

7 W.P. Ward, *White Canada Forever: Popular Attitudes and Public Policy toward Orientals in British Columbia* (Montreal, 1978), 110-12 and 119-23

8 Young and Reid, *The Japanese Canadians*, 98-9

9 On the history of the anti-Oriental movements in British Columbia see Ward, *White Canada Forever, passim*.

10 Ward, *White Canada Forever*, 142-66

11 On the relocation of the Japanese see F.E. LaViolette, *The Canadian Japanese and World War II: A Sociological and Psychological Account* (Toronto, 1948), 56-201

12 LaViolette, *The Canadian Japanese*, 92-4; Adachi, *The Enemy That Never Was*, 242-3

13 LaViolette, *The Canadian Japanese*, 226-74; Adachi, *The Enemy That Never Was*, 296-319